Must Habits

Must Habits

The Identity-First System for
Building Habits Across All 7 Life Domains

═══

STEPHEN RUE

Award Winning, Best Selling Author

The Must Personal Development Book Series:

Must: Becoming the Person You Are Meant to Be
Must Goals: The Art and Science of Authentic Goal-Setting for Lasting Change
Must Habits: The Identity-First System for Building Habits Across All 7 Life Domains
Must Year: Your Best Year of Becoming – A 365-Day Journey of Identity, Growth, and Habits
Must Book Guided Journal: Daily Prompts for Personal Development, Self-Improvement, and Growth for Success

For a listing of all books in the *Must* Series, go to MustHabits.com

MUST BOOK PRESS
COPYRIGHT © 2026 Stephen Rue
All rights reserved.

Must Habits: The Identity-First System for Building Habits Across All 7 Life Domains

FIRST EDITION

ISBN: 979-8-9944215-2-9   Hardback
ISBN: 979-8-9944215-3-6   Paperback
ISBN: 979-8-9944215-4-3   E-Book

For more resources, visit MustHabits.com

CONTENTS

Introduction: The Identity Revolution xi

PART I: THE FOUNDATION

Chapter 1: Why Goals Die (And How Identity Saves Them) 1
Chapter 2: I AM Statements—The Core of Change 11
Chapter 3: The Must Circle of Life 24

PART II: THE SCIENCE

Chapter 4: Living in the Must Zone 39
Chapter 5: The Must Habit Loop—How Change Happens 51
Chapter 6: The Truth About 66 Days 64

PART III: THE TEMPLATES

Chapter 7: Health, Relationships & Career Habits 79
Chapter 8: Finance, Growth, Spirit & Legacy Habits 91

PART IV: ADVANCED STRATEGIES

Chapter 9: When You Break the Streak 107
Chapter 10: Environment Design & Advanced Tactics 115
Chapter 11: The Complete Must Habits System 124

Conclusion: Your Transformation Begins Today 135

APPENDICES

Appendix A: The Must Habits Toolkit 143
Appendix B: Quick Reference Guide 160
Appendix C: Troubleshooting Guide... 163
Appendix D: Resources and References 166

About the Author 181
Acknowledgments 183
A Final Word.. 185
References & Ongoing Research Updates 187
Thank you, and Next Steps 189
The Must Personal Development Series 191

This Book Is Different—and It's Built for You

"You don't get in life what you want, you get in life what you are."

— Les Brown

Most habit books promise big change and deliver clever tips. This one gives you a complete, identity-based system you can actually live with for the rest of your life.

You are not failing because you are weak, lazy, undisciplined, or "just not a habits person." You are failing because you have been handed behavior-based advice for identity-level problems. You have tried:

- Forcing yourself to "just be consistent" until your willpower collapsed.
- 21- or 30-day challenges that fizzled out as soon as life got busy.
- Affirmations that sounded powerful but secretly made you feel like a fraud.
- Habit trackers and apps that helped for a week, then gathered dust.

If that sounds familiar, this book is for you.

Must Habits is built on a simple but radical shift: you do not start with what you want to do; you start with who you are becoming. Instead of stacking random behaviors, you will:

- Define clear, evidence-based I AM Statements that describe your real identity in each area of life.
- Turn those identities into Must Actions—the nonnegotiable habits that prove who you are every day.

- Run those habits through the Must Habit Loop: a precise sequence (Signal → Identity Reminder → Tiny Action → Evidence/Celebration) that encodes them in your brain.

Yes, you will see some of the same core science that appears in other excellent books—habit loops, the truth about 66 days, why willpower fails, and how the brain wires new routines. Science is science. But how that science is framed and implemented determines whether your life actually changes. This is where this book is different:

- Identity is not a side note; it is the foundation. Every habit begins with who you are, not what you want.
- The 66-day research is not a trivia fact; it becomes a lived roadmap—Honeymoon, Grind, Integration—so you know exactly what to expect and how to push through when motivation dies.
- The habit loop is not a diagram on a page; it becomes a four-step checklist you will run in real time, tied directly to your I AM Statement and your daily proof.

Most books ask you to build habits in isolation. Must Habits refuses to treat your life that way. You will work across seven interconnected domains—health, relationships, career, finances, growth, spirituality, and legacy—using the Must Circle of Life to see where you are strong, where you are struggling, and where a single new habit will create the greatest ripple effect. You will not guess which habit to build next; you will use proven templates and clear 90-day roadmaps so every action fits inside a bigger story.

This book also understands what actually happens after the first week. It anticipates your real pain points:

- "I broke my streak—now what?" You will learn the Two-Day Rule and emergency mini-habits so one bad day never becomes the death of a habit.

- "Life just exploded—I can't do my full routine." You will learn how to shrink habits without breaking identity, preserving your sense of self even in crisis.
- "I've changed before, then slid back." You will learn how to turn habits into visible, daily proof so your brain stops clinging to the old story about who you are.

Finally, Must Habits does not stand alone. It is the habit volume inside the larger Must personal development ecosystem. If you have already begun clarifying your Must Purpose and Must Goals, this book will give you the daily operating system to live them. If you are starting here, it will still work—every chapter is designed to stand on its own—but you will also see how your new habits can connect to a bigger, coherent path.

The promise of this book is simple and honest:

If you will commit to one identity, one Must Habit Loop, and one 90-day stretch at a time, you will no longer be someone "trying to change." You will become the person whose daily actions finally match the life you know you are meant to live.

INTRODUCTION

The Identity Revolution

Sarah stared at her gym membership card.

Three years. $1,800. Twelve visits.

She'd tried everything—early morning workouts, evening classes, personal trainers, fitness apps, motivational playlists, workout buddies. Each January brought renewed determination. Each February brought familiar defeat.

The problem wasn't willpower. Sarah crushed it at work, led a team of fifteen, managed complex projects with precision. She had discipline in spades.

The problem was her approach.

She was trying to build a behavior (go to the gym) without changing her identity (who she believed she was).

In her mind, she was "someone trying to get fit." Every workout required convincing herself to act against her identity. Every missed session confirmed who she really was—someone who didn't exercise.

Then something shifted.

After reading Must: Becoming the Person You're Meant to Be, Sarah stopped trying to force behaviors and started with a different question: Who do I need to become?

Her answer: "I am someone who honors my body through movement."

Not "I want to work out." Not "I should exercise." Not "I'm trying to get fit."

I AM someone who moves.

That identity shift changed everything.

She didn't start with intense workouts. She started with tiny actions that proved her new identity: putting on workout clothes each morning, doing five pushups before coffee, walking to the far parking spot.

Each action wasn't about fitness. It was about identity. Each day she showed up—even for just five minutes—she cast another vote for the person she was becoming.

Ninety days later, exercise wasn't something she forced herself to do. It was simply who she was.

The Crisis Most People Don't See

Sarah's story isn't unique. It's epidemic.

Every year, millions of people set goals. They commit to meditation, healthy eating, daily writing, financial discipline, quality time with family. They download apps, buy planners, hire coaches, join accountability groups.

And 92% of them fail.

Not because they lack discipline. Not because they don't want it badly enough. Not because they didn't try hard enough.

They fail because they're using a behavior-based approach to habit formation. They're trying to force actions without shifting identity. And behavior-based change doesn't last.

Here's why:

- Behavior change requires constant willpower. You're always fighting yourself, convincing yourself, forcing yourself. Willpower depletes. The habit breaks.
- Behavior change creates internal conflict. When your identity says "I'm not a runner" but you're trying to run daily, every run feels like betrayal. You snap back to who you believe you are.
- Behavior change is fragile. One disruption—vacation, illness, stress—and the habit shatters. You have no foundation to return to because the behavior was never rooted in identity.

There's a better way.

What Makes Must Habits Different

This book flips the script.

Instead of asking "What should I do?" you'll start with "Who do I need to become?"

Must Habits is the habit system that makes identity its foundation, not a side note.

Must Habits is the fully integrated identity-first system across seven life domains

While other books mention identity as one component among many, we make it the foundation. Everything flows from who you are.

Here's what makes this approach different:

- Identity-first framework. Every habit begins with an I AM Statement. You define who you're becoming, then choose behaviors that prove that identity. The actions flow naturally from the identity instead of fighting against it.
- The Must Circle of Life. Unlike books that treat all habits equally, we show you how to build habits across seven interconnected life domains—health, relationships, career, finances, growth, spirituality, and legacy. Life isn't one-dimensional. Your habits shouldn't be either.
- Integration with the Must ecosystem. This book is part of a complete transformation system. You've defined your Must Purpose in Book 1. Now you build the daily habits to live it. Next, you'll set Must Goals to expand it. Three books, one cohesive path.
- Scientifically accurate timelines. We don't sell you myths about 21-day habit formation. The research shows it takes an average of 66 days to build automaticity—and we'll show you exactly how to navigate that timeline.
- Practical, ready-to-use templates. You don't have to guess which habits to build. We give you 19 complete habit templates across all seven life domains, each designed with the full Must Habit Loop. Pick one, commit for 90 days, transform.

How to Use This Book

This isn't a book you'll read once and shelve. It's a system you'll use for the rest of your life.

Here's how to get the most from it:

Read it sequentially first.

Part I builds your foundation—why identity matters, how to create I AM Statements, and how to assess your life domains. Part II explains the science—the habit loop, the neuroscience of change, and realistic timelines. Part III gives you templates. Part IV shows you advanced strategies and how to build a complete system.

Start with one habit.

The temptation will be to build five habits simultaneously. Don't. Choose one domain (your weakest spoke in the Must Circle of Life), select one habit from the templates, and commit to 90 days. Master one before adding another.

Use the tools and assessments.

Throughout this book, you'll find worksheets, trackers, and assessment tools. Don't skip them. The Must Circle of Life Assessment shows you where to start. The Habit Loop Builder helps you design your first habit. The 90-Day Tracker keeps you accountable. These aren't optional extras—they're essential components of the system.

Pay attention to the science sidebars.

If you're analytically minded, you'll appreciate the neuroscience sidebars explaining why the system works at a brain level. If you're not, skip them. The system works either way.

Return to this book as a reference.

Once you master your first habit, come back and build your second. Then your third. Over time, you'll build habits across all seven life domains, creating a complete system of daily proof for the person you're becoming.

What's Ahead

In the chapters that follow, you'll discover:

- Why most habit advice fails (and why identity-based change succeeds)

- How to create powerful I AM Statements that drive lasting transformation
- The Must Circle of Life assessment to identify your weakest domain
- The exact 4-step habit loop that makes behaviors automatic
- The truth about 66-day habit formation (including the "grind" that most people quit during)
- 19 complete habit templates across health, relationships, career, finances, growth, spirit, and legacy
- The Two-Day Rule that prevents broken streaks from becoming habit death
- Advanced strategies like environment design, temptation bundling, and keystone habits
- A complete system for building habits that compound into transformation

The journey from behavior-based struggle to identity-based transformation begins now.

You're not trying to force new behaviors. You're becoming someone new.

And that changes everything.

PART I
THE FOUNDATION

CHAPTER 1

Why Goals Die (And How Identity Saves Them)

We are what we repeatedly do.
Excellence, then, is not an act, but a habit.
— *Aristotle (via Will Durant)*

Marcus had a spreadsheet.

Sixty-three rows. Every goal he'd set in the past five years, color-coded by category: green for health, blue for career, purple for relationships, yellow for finances.

Achievement rate? 11%.

It wasn't for lack of trying. Marcus was disciplined. He set SMART goals, created action plans, tracked progress religiously. Each January brought a fresh list. Each December brought the same disappointing pattern: a few wins, many losses, and that familiar feeling of falling short.

The problem wasn't the goals. It was the approach.

Marcus was focused on outcomes—lose 20 pounds, get promoted, save $10,000. These were destinations. But he had no vehicle to get there. No system. No daily proof. Just willpower, which worked great... until it didn't.

Then he discovered something that changed everything: his goals were dying because they weren't rooted in his identity.

He wasn't trying to become a healthy person. He was trying to lose weight. He wasn't building the habits of a financially disciplined person. He was chasing a number. The goals were external targets, disconnected from who he was.

So he flipped it.

Instead of "I want to lose 20 pounds," he started with "I am someone who honors my body through movement and nutrition." Instead of "I need to save $10,000," he declared "I am financially disciplined."

The shift seemed subtle. The results were not.

Eighteen months later, Marcus had lost 35 pounds, saved $18,000, and earned his promotion. More importantly, exercise felt automatic. Budgeting felt natural. Excellence at work felt like baseline.

Patricia had the same New Year's resolution for seven consecutive years: lose 30 pounds. Every January 1st brought renewed hope. She'd buy a gym membership, stock the fridge with vegetables, download a calorie-tracking app. The first week felt electric with possibility.

By February, the gym bag gathered dust. By March, the vegetables rotted in the crisper. By April, she'd deleted the app. Every year, same pattern. Same disappointment. Same shame.

The breaking point came on her eighth January 1st. Standing in front of the mirror, she realized she'd now spent seven years "trying to lose weight" and was actually 15 pounds heavier than when she started. The definition of insanity, she thought bitterly.

Then Patricia discovered the identity-first approach. Instead of setting a weight-loss goal, she created one I AM Statement: "I am someone who nourishes my body." Her Must Action wasn't "lose 30 pounds." It was: drink 64 ounces of water daily. That's it. No calorie counting. No intense workouts. Just water.

Eighteen months later, Patricia had lost 42 pounds. But the real transformation was internal. She no longer saw herself as someone "trying to lose weight." She was someone who nourished her body. And that person made completely different choices about food, movement, and self-care.

Because he wasn't chasing outcomes anymore. He was living as his identity.

The Problem With Goals

Every January, millions of people set goals with genuine hope. They declare this will be the year they transform their health, advance their careers, improve their relationships, finally achieve financial freedom.

By February, 92% of those goals are abandoned.

Why? Not because people lack ambition. Not because they don't care. Because they're using the wrong vehicle.

Goals are destinations. Habits are the vehicle that gets you there.

And when your habits are rooted in identity—when they flow from who you are rather than what you want—they become unstoppable. They become what we call Must Actions: the nonnegotiable behaviors that define you.

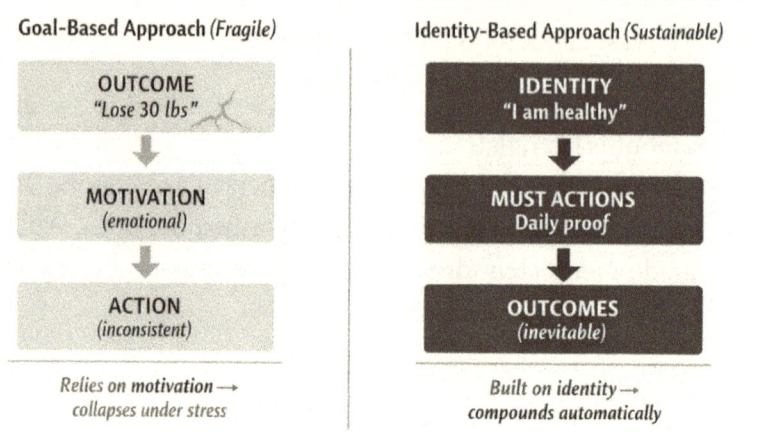

Six Reasons Goals Fail (And Habits Succeed)

1. Motivation Fades, But Systems Persist

Goals depend on motivation, and motivation is unstable. It surges when you're inspired, crashes when you're tired, disappears when life gets hard.

Habits don't require motivation. Once established, they run on autopilot. You don't need to feel motivated to brush your teeth. You just do it.

When your habits become Must Actions—behaviors aligned with your core identity—they're even more powerful. They're not just automatic; they're essential. You do them because they're who you are, not because you feel like it.

THE NEUROSCIENCE: Why Willpower Isn't the Answer

It's tempting to believe that willpower "runs out" like a muscle, but modern research suggests something more nuanced is happening.

What undermines consistency is not a depleted resource, but **decision fatigue, cognitive load, and motivation volatility.**

Throughout the day, your brain is forced to make thousands of micro-decisions. Each one competes for attention, energy, and emotional regulation. By the time evening arrives—or stress spikes—your capacity to choose effortful behaviors drops sharply. Not because willpower is gone, but because the system is overloaded.

This is why successful habits are not built on motivation or self-control. They are built on **design**—clear signals, identity reminders, tiny actions, and automatic reinforcement. When the environment and identity do the work, consistency no longer depends on how you feel.

2. Goals Lack Identity, Habits Encode It

Most goals are outcome-focused: "Lose 30 pounds." "Earn $100,000." "Run a marathon." These are destinations, but they don't tell you who you need to become.

Habits, when designed correctly, encode identity into daily life. Instead of "I want to lose weight," you build the habits of someone who is healthy: meal prepping, walking after dinner, choosing protein.

Every time you perform a habit aligned with your identity, you cast a vote for the person you're becoming.

As James Clear writes in Atomic Habits: "Every action you take is a vote for the type of person you wish to become."

3. Goals End, Habits Continue

What happens when you achieve a goal? You celebrate briefly, then you're back to square one. You lost the weight, but now what? You hit the sales target, but what about next month?

This is the finish-line problem: goals have endings, but life doesn't. When you focus solely on the outcome, you stop the behaviors that got you there as soon as you arrive.

Habits solve this. When your focus is on the daily practice—the system, not the destination—you don't stop when you hit a milestone. The habit is the victory. The outcome is just a pleasant side effect.

4. Overwhelm Paralyzes, Small Actions Compound

Big goals are inspiring, but they're also overwhelming. "Write a book" sounds impossible when you're staring at a blank page. "Get out of debt" feels crushing when you owe six figures.

Overwhelm leads to paralysis. When the goal feels too big, we don't know where to start, so we don't start at all.

Habits break the goal into tiny actions. Instead of "write a book," you write 300 words every morning. Instead of "get out of debt," you automatically transfer $50 to savings every payday.

These actions feel manageable, and over time, they compound into extraordinary results.

5. Willpower Depletes, But Identity Endures

Willpower is unreliable under cognitive load and emotional stress. Research shows that making decisions, resisting temptations, and forcing yourself to do difficult things all drain from the same cognitive tank.

But identity doesn't deplete. When a behavior is tied to who you are—when you can say "I am a writer" or "I am someone who keeps commitments"—you don't need willpower to act. You're simply being yourself.

6. Misalignment Creates Resistance, Alignment Creates Flow

This is the most critical reason goals fail: they're not aligned with your core self. You set goals based on what you think you should want, what others expect, or what looks impressive.

But if a goal doesn't resonate with your Must Values and Must Purpose, you'll sabotage it subconsciously. Your conscious mind says 'Do this,' but your unconscious mind resists.

When your habits are aligned with who you truly are—when they're Must Actions flowing from your Must Identity—there's no resistance. There's flow. You're not forcing yourself to be someone else; you're simply living as yourself.

Must Actions: Habits That Define You

Not all habits are created equal. Some are maintenance routines—brushing your teeth, making your bed, checking email. These are useful, but they're not transformative.

Then there are Must Actions: the habits so aligned with your core identity, values, and purpose that not doing them would feel like betraying yourself.

Must Actions are the deliberate, nonnegotiable behaviors that drive you forward, even when challenges arise.

Must Actions are not optional. They are essential. They are the daily proof that you are who you say you are.

Examples:

- If you've declared "I am a writer," then writing every day is a Must Action.
- If you've declared "I am a present, loving parent," then putting away your phone during family dinner is a Must Action.

- If you're financially disciplined, then reviewing your budget weekly is a Must Action.
- If you take care of your body, then moving daily is a Must Action.

These aren't just good ideas. They're identity requirements. When you skip them, you experience cognitive dissonance—a gap between who you say you are and how you're actually living.

EXAMPLE: From Behavior to Identity

Jennifer struggled with daily meditation for three years. She knew it was "good for her," tried various apps, set morning alarms, joined challenges. Nothing stuck.

The shift came when she stopped trying to "meditate daily" and started with identity: "I am someone who cultivates inner peace."

That identity demanded Must Actions: sit in silence each morning, even for 60 seconds. Not because meditation was a goal. Because inner peace was who she was.

Six months later, meditation was as automatic as brushing teeth. Why? Because it proved her identity.

The Paradigm Shift

Here's the shift this book will help you make:

Old way:

"I want to lose 30 pounds, so I'll diet until I hit that number."

New way:

"I am someone who nourishes my body and moves regularly. Weight loss is a side effect of who I am."

Old way:

"I want to be successful, so I'll work hard until I achieve success."

New way:

"I am someone who shows up with excellence every day. Success is inevitable."

Old way:

"I want better relationships, so I'll try to be more present."

New way:

"I am a present, connected person. My relationships thrive because of who I am."

The difference is subtle but seismic. In the old way, you're chasing an outcome. In the new way, you're living as your identity. The outcome happens naturally.

Proof Over Promises

Your brain doesn't believe what you tell it. It believes what you show it.

You can declare "I am a runner" all you want, but if you never run, your brain won't buy it. Identity isn't established through affirmations alone. It's established through repeated proof.

Every time you perform a Must Action, you're providing evidence to yourself and the world that you are who you claim to be.

This is why habits are so powerful: they turn identity from an aspiration into a reality. They make who you are visible, tangible, and undeniable.

Examples of daily proof:

- When you wake up at 5:00 AM to write, you prove you're a writer
- When you meal prep on Sunday, you prove you value your health
- When you put your phone away during dinner, you prove you're a present parent
- When you track your expenses daily, you prove you're financially disciplined

Each action is a vote. Each day is an election. And when you vote consistently for the same identity, you win.

What's Coming in Chapter 2

This chapter established the foundation: goals die, but habits live forever—especially when those habits are rooted in identity and aligned with your Must Values and Must Purpose.

In the next chapter, we'll get practical. You'll learn how to craft I AM Statements—the precise declarations of identity that serve as the foundation for all your Must Actions.

These aren't vague affirmations. They're clear, specific, actionable statements that tell you exactly who you are and what that identity demands of you daily.

By the time you finish Chapter 2, you'll have a complete identity framework that makes building habits almost automatic.

Goals are what you want.

Habits are who you are.

And who you are always wins.

CHAPTER 2

I AM Statements—The Core of Change

*The statements we make about ourselves,
beginning with "I am," are incredibly powerful.*
— From Must: Becoming the Person You Are Meant to Be

David stared at the sticky note on his bathroom mirror.

"I am confident. I am successful. I am wealthy."

He'd been repeating these affirmations for six months. Every morning, he recited them with conviction. Every evening, he felt like a fraud.

Because the truth was: he wasn't confident. His hands shook before presentations. He wasn't successful—not by his definition. And he definitely wasn't wealthy. The affirmations didn't inspire him. They reminded him of the gap between who he wanted to be and who he actually was.

Angela spent two years telling herself "I will become fit" and "I am going to love exercise." Every Monday she'd start fresh. By Thursday, the gym bag sat untouched in her car. The affirmations felt hollow because her brain knew they weren't true yet.

Then Angela discovered the power of present-tense identity. Instead of declaring a future state, she identified one tiny behavior she could prove today: "I am someone who moves daily." Not "will be athletic someday." Just: I move my body every single day.

The shift was subtle but profound. On day one, she walked to her mailbox and back—sixty seconds. That was enough to prove the identity. On day three, she did ten jumping jacks in her kitchen. Day twelve, she walked around the block. Each action, no matter how small, reinforced the same truth.

Ninety days later, Angela was working out five days a week. But more importantly, she no longer saw exercise as something she "should do" or "will do eventually." She had become someone who moves. The behavior followed the identity, not the other way around.

The problem wasn't the concept. It was the execution.

Affirmations ask you to declare what isn't true yet. They create cognitive dissonance—your brain knows you're lying. Instead of building identity, they highlight the gap.

Then David learned about I AM Statements.

Instead of declaring a future fantasy, he described his current identity based on daily proof:

"I am someone who shows up prepared. I practice my presentations. I honor my commitments."

This was true. He could prove it. His brain accepted it.

And when he acted from that identity—when he showed up prepared, practiced diligently, honored commitments—confidence emerged naturally. Not as an affirmation. As a side effect of identity.

The Power of "I AM"

In Must Goals, you discovered the I AM SMART TO ACT™ Goals Method, which places identity—your I AM—at the very center of goal achievement. This isn't motivational rhetoric. It's supported by decades of research in psychology and neuroscience.

Every "I am" statement you declare, whether conscious or not, crystallizes part of your identity and directs your behavior.

When you say "I am a writer," "I am resilient," or "I am a present parent," you're not just describing yourself—you're reinforcing neural pathways that make those identities real.

The inverse is also true. When you say "I am terrible with money," "I am not a morning person," or "I am bad at relationships," you create self-fulfilling prophecies. Your brain believes what you repeatedly tell it.

For fifteen years, James introduced himself as "terrible with money." He'd laugh about it at dinner parties—"I'm just not a numbers guy." His friends nodded knowingly. His wife stopped asking him to handle bills. The identity became armor protecting him from having to change.

The wake-up call came at 43 when his financial advisor showed him the retirement projections: at his current trajectory, he'd work until 75. Maybe longer. "You're not bad with money," the advisor said flatly. "You've just convinced yourself you are."

James realized he'd spent fifteen years proving his limiting identity true. Every overdraft fee, every impulse purchase, every ignored credit card statement reinforced: "See? I'm bad with money." His brain had found exactly the evidence it was looking for.

He created a new identity: "I am someone who tracks every dollar." Not "good with money"—too vague. Not "financially free"—too far away. Just: I track every dollar. Day one, he logged three transactions in a notebook. Day seven, he reviewed his weekly spending. Day thirty, he saw patterns he'd never noticed before.

Eighteen months later, James had paid off $23,000 in credit card debt and saved $15,000. But the real transformation was internal. He no longer identified as "bad with money." He was someone who tracked every dollar. And that person made very different choices.

The Identity Proof Loop

THE NEUROSCIENCE: How Identity Forms in the Brain

Your self-concept lives in a network of neural connections across multiple brain regions—particularly the medial prefrontal cortex. Every time you think "I am X," you activate and strengthen those connections.

Your brain then seeks evidence to confirm that identity through confirmation bias—noticing information that supports your self-concept while filtering out contradictory data. This is why identity-based habits work: they provide consistent evidence that your brain uses to strengthen the neural networks of your desired identity.

I AM Statements vs. Affirmations: The Critical Difference

Most people confuse I AM Statements with affirmations, but they're fundamentally different:

Affirmations are aspirational:

"I am wealthy" (when you're in debt)

"I am confident" (when you feel insecure)

"I am successful" (when you're struggling)

These create cognitive dissonance. Your brain knows they're not true, so it rejects them. Worse, they can make you feel like a fraud, widening the gap between who you say you are and who you actually are.

I AM Statements are rooted in current reality and proven by daily behavior:

"I am someone who manages money wisely" (proven by tracking expenses)

"I am becoming more confident" (proven by taking small risks)

"I am building success daily" (proven by consistent action)

The difference is honesty and evidence. I AM Statements don't lie about where you are. They declare who you're being right now, even if you're still becoming who you want to be.

The Four Characteristics of Effective I AM Statements

1. Present Tense (Not Future)

I AM Statements declare who you are NOW, not who you hope to become.

Weak: "I will be healthy."

Strong: "I am someone who takes care of my body."

The first is a promise. The second is an identity. Present tense creates urgency and accountability.

2. Identity-Focused (Not Outcome-Focused)

I AM Statements describe WHO you are, not WHAT you want.

Weak: "I am going to run a marathon."

Strong: "I am a runner."

Outcomes are targets. Identity is sustainable. When you are a runner, running marathons is just what you do.

3. Action-Oriented (Provable Through Behavior)

I AM Statements must be demonstrable through daily Must Actions.

Weak: "I am successful."

Strong: "I am someone who shows up with excellence every day."

The first is vague. The second gives you a daily standard to meet. Every day you show up with excellence, you prove the statement true.

4. Specific to Life Areas (Aligned with Must Circle of Life)

As you learned in Must and Must Goals, the Must Circle of Life has seven key domains:

- Health & Vitality
- Relationships & Love
- Career & Professional Development
- Financial Well-Being
- Personal Growth & Learning

- Spiritual and Peace of Mind
- Community & Legacy

Effective I AM Statements are specific to these areas. You don't just have ONE identity—you have an identity in each domain that matters to you.

How to Construct Your I AM Statements

Here's a simple three-step process for crafting I AM Statements for each area of your Must Circle of Life:

Step 1: Choose Your Life Area

Select one domain from the Must Circle of Life where you want to build Must Habits. Start with the area that feels most urgent or where you're experiencing the most misalignment.

For example: Health & Vitality

Step 2: Identify Your Core Values in That Area

From Must Goals, you learned to select three Must Core Values for each life domain. These are your "keywords"—the principles that guide all your decisions in that area.

For Health & Vitality, your values might be: Energy, Consistency, Self-Respect

Step 3: Write Your I AM Statement

Combine your values into a present-tense declaration that describes who you are in this domain.

Formula: "I am [identity] who [specific behaviors that prove it]."

Example:

"I am someone who honors my body with consistent movement, nutritious food, and adequate rest because I value energy, consistency, and self-respect."

I AM Statement Examples Across the Must Circle of Life

Here are examples of strong I AM Statements for each domain:

Health & Vitality

"I am someone who treats my body as the vehicle for my purpose. I move daily, nourish myself with intention, and prioritize rest because vitality fuels everything I do."

Relationships & Love

"I am a present, loving partner who creates deep connection through quality time, honest communication, and consistent acts of care."

Career & Professional Development

"I am a professional who shows up with excellence, continuously develops my skills, and adds value to every project I touch."

Financial Well-Being

"I am financially disciplined. I track my spending, invest consistently, and make decisions aligned with long-term security and freedom."

Personal Growth & Learning

"I am a lifelong learner who dedicates time daily to reading, reflection, and skill development because growth is my default state."

Spiritual and Peace of Mind

"I am someone who cultivates inner peace through daily meditation, prayer, and gratitude because my spiritual health grounds everything else."

Community & Legacy

"I am a contributor who serves my community, mentors others, and builds a legacy of positive impact through consistent acts of generosity and leadership."

From I AM Statements to Must Actions

Here's where I AM Statements become powerful: they naturally generate Must Actions.

Once you've declared "I am someone who honors my body with consistent movement," the Must Action is obvious: move your body daily. It's not optional. It's not negotiable. It's who you are.

This is the bridge between identity and behavior that makes habit formation almost automatic. When you know who you are, you know what you must do.

Your I AM Statements declare the identity. Your Must Actions prove it.

The Identity Proof Loop

Here's how I AM Statements and Must Actions work together:

1. You declare your I AM Statement: "I am a writer."
2. That identity demands a Must Action: Write daily.
3. You perform the Must Action: You write 500 words this morning.
4. The action provides proof: You have evidence you're a writer.
5. The proof strengthens the identity: "I really am a writer."
6. The strengthened identity makes the next Must Action easier.

This is the Identity Proof Loop. Every time you complete the loop, your identity becomes more real, your habits become more automatic, and your transformation becomes inevitable.

When Identity and Action Don't Match

What happens when you declare "I am a writer" but don't write? Cognitive dissonance.

Your brain experiences discomfort when your stated identity and actual behavior don't align. You have two options:

- Option 1: Change the behavior to match the identity (start writing)
- Option 2: Change the identity to match the behavior (stop calling yourself a writer)

Most people take option two. They lower their identity to match their behavior. They stop declaring who they want to be and settle for who they currently are.

But when you build your I AM Statements properly—when they're rooted in your Must Values and aligned with your Must Purpose—option two becomes unacceptable. You must take option one. You must act.

This is the power of identity-driven habits. The discomfort of NOT acting becomes greater than the discomfort of acting.

EXAMPLE: The Power of Cognitive Dissonance

Rachel declared "I am someone who maintains a clean, organized living space." For the first week, nothing changed. Dishes piled up. Laundry overflowed.

But the cognitive dissonance was unbearable. Every time she walked past the mess, her brain screamed: "This doesn't match who you said you are."

By week two, she couldn't stand it anymore. She started doing dishes immediately after meals. She put laundry away the same day. Not because she felt motivated. Because NOT doing it felt worse than doing it.

The identity created the discomfort. The discomfort drove the action. The action proved the identity.

Your I AM Statements Evolve

I AM Statements are not static. As you grow, they should grow with you.

What was true six months ago may not be true today. What challenges you today may be effortless next year.

This is healthy evolution, not inconsistency. You're not abandoning who you are—you're becoming more of who you're meant to be.

Review your I AM Statements quarterly. Ask yourself:

- Is this still true?
- Does this still serve my Must Purpose?
- Am I providing consistent proof through my actions?
- Is it time to raise the standard?

For example: "I am someone who moves my body three times per week" might evolve into "I am an athlete who trains six days per week." Both are true at different stages. Neither is better. Both serve you where you are.

Creating Your First I AM Statement

Before moving to Chapter 3, take a moment to create one I AM Statement.

Choose one domain from the Must Circle of Life—the area where building strong habits would have the greatest impact on your life right now.

If you've completed Must Goals, you already know your three Must Core Values in that domain. If not, choose the three values that feel most essential to who you want to be in this area.

Write your I AM Statement using the formula: "I am [identity] who [behaviors] because [values]." Make it present tense, identity-focused, action-oriented, and provable.

Then identify one Must Action that proves this identity. What is the single most important behavior that demonstrates you are who you say you are?

This is your foundation. In the next chapter, you'll learn how to apply this process across all seven domains of the Must Circle of Life.

What's Coming in Chapter 3

You now understand that identity drives behavior and I AM Statements define identity. But how do you decide WHICH identities to focus on? How do you balance habits across the different areas of your life?

That's where the Must Circle of Life comes in—the framework that ensures you're not just building habits, but building a complete, balanced, purposeful life.

In Chapter 3, you'll learn how to apply I AM Statements and Must Actions across all seven life domains so you can thrive holistically, not just in isolated areas.

Who You Say You Are Matters.

But Who You Prove You Are Through Daily Action?

That's Everything.

CHAPTER 3

The Must Circle of Life

I believe that being successful means having a balance of success stories across the many areas of your life.
— Zig Ziglar

Elena was crushing it.

At 34, she was the youngest VP at her firm. Six-figure salary. Corner office. Industry recognition. Her career segment of the Must Circle of Life was a perfect 10/10.

Everything else was a 2.

Her marriage was on life support—three months since she'd had a real conversation with her husband. Her health was declining—stress-eating, no exercise, constant exhaustion. Her friendships had evaporated. She couldn't remember the last time she read a book for pleasure or sat in silence for more than 30 seconds.

From the outside, Elena was successful. From the inside, she was collapsing.

The breaking point came during her annual review. Her boss asked: 'Elena, you're phenomenal at work. How's everything else?'

She couldn't answer. Because she didn't know. She'd been so laser-focused on career excellence that she'd forgotten to check if the rest of her life still existed.

That evening, she completed the Must Circle of Life assessment.

The results were brutal:

- Career: 10/10
- Health: 2/10
- Relationships: 3/10
- Finances: 8/10 (good income, poor management)
- Growth: 1/10
- Spiritual: 1/10
- Legacy: 2/10

The wheel was broken. And she could feel it.

Elena didn't need another promotion. She needed balance. She didn't need to work harder. She needed to build habits in the domains she'd neglected.

Eighteen months later, her Circle of Life looked completely different. Career was still strong (8/10—she learned she didn't need to be perfect). But Health was 7/10. Relationships 8/10. Growth 6/10. Spiritual 7/10.

The wheel rolled smoothly. And for the first time in years, success felt sustainable.

Why Most People Fail at Balance

You now know that habits rooted in identity are powerful. You've learned how to craft I AM Statements that define who you are. But here's the critical question: WHERE should you focus your habit-building energy?

Most people make one of two mistakes:

Mistake #1: They try to build habits in every area simultaneously. They commit to exercise, meditation, journaling, budgeting, date nights, skill development, and volunteering—all at once. Within two weeks, they're overwhelmed. Within a month, everything collapses.

Mistake #2: They hyper-focus on one area while neglecting everything else. Usually career or health. They optimize one domain brilliantly while the other six deteriorate. They achieve success... but it feels hollow.

Both approaches fail because they ignore a fundamental truth: your life is not one-dimensional. You are not just a professional, or a parent, or an athlete. You are all of these things, and more.

This is where the Must Circle of Life becomes essential.

Understanding the Must Circle of Life

The Must Circle of Life is a holistic framework for evaluating and balancing the major areas of your life.

Think of it as a wheel with seven spokes, each representing a critical life domain. When all seven spokes are strong, the wheel rolls smoothly. When even one spoke is weak or broken, the entire wheel wobbles.

The framework originated with personal development pioneers like Zig Ziglar and Paul J. Meyer in the 1960s, and it remains one of the most powerful self-assessment tools in coaching and personal growth.

The Must Circle of Life

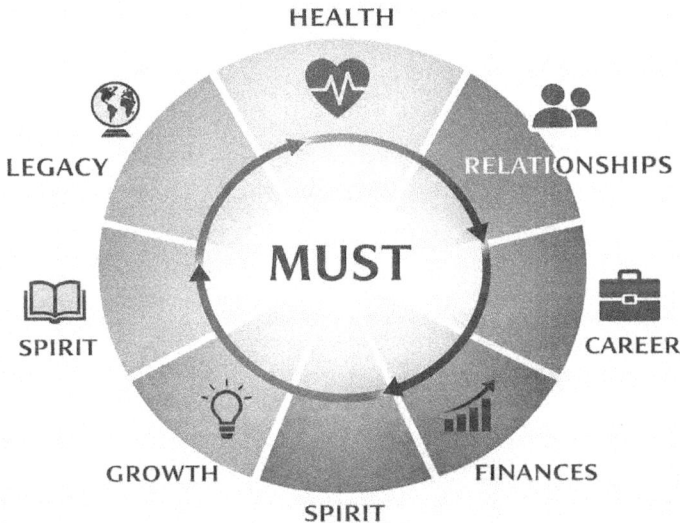

The Seven Elements of the Must Circle of Life

Let's explore each domain and understand what it means to build Must Habits in that area:

1. Health & Vitality

This is the foundation. Without health, everything else suffers. This domain includes physical fitness, nutrition, sleep, energy management, and preventive care.

> *I AM Statement example:* "I am someone who honors my body as the vehicle for my purpose through consistent movement, nutritious food, and adequate rest."
>
> *Must Action example:* Move your body for at least 30 minutes daily.

2. Relationships & Love

Humans are social beings. This domain covers romantic partnerships, family connections, friendships, and your broader social network. Relationships are where meaning lives.

> *I AM Statement example:* "I am a present, loving partner who creates deep connection through quality time, honest communication, and consistent acts of care."
>
> *Must Action example:* Have one distraction-free conversation with your partner daily.

3. Career & Professional Development

This includes your work, professional growth, skill development, and the pursuit of mastery in your field. It's about contribution and competence.

> *I AM Statement example:* "I am a professional who shows up with excellence, continuously develops my skills, and adds measurable value to every project."
>
> *Must Action example:* Dedicate 30 minutes daily to skill development or deep work.

4. Financial Well-Being

This domain covers earning, saving, investing, debt management, and creating financial security and freedom. Money doesn't buy happiness—but financial stress destroys it.

> *I AM Statement example:* "I am financially disciplined. I track my spending, invest consistently, and make decisions aligned with long-term security."

Must Action example: Review your budget and track expenses weekly.

5. Personal Growth & Learning

Continuous learning and self-development. This includes reading, education, new experiences, and the intentional pursuit of wisdom. Growth is not optional—stagnation is decline.

> *I AM Statement example:* "I am a lifelong learner who dedicates time daily to reading, reflection, and expanding my understanding because growth is my default state."
>
> *Must Action example:* Read or listen to educational content for 20 minutes daily.

6. Spiritual and Peace of Mind

This domain encompasses your spiritual practices, inner peace, meditation, prayer, mindfulness, and your relationship with something larger than yourself. Without inner peace, external success feels empty.

> *I AM Statement example:* "I am someone who cultivates inner peace through daily meditation, prayer, and gratitude because my spiritual health grounds everything else."
>
> *Must Action example:* Practice meditation, prayer, or gratitude journaling for 10 minutes each morning.

7. Community & Legacy

This is about contribution beyond yourself—service, mentorship, volunteering, and the impact you leave on the world. Legacy is what remains when you're gone.

> *I AM Statement example:* "I am a contributor who serves my community, mentors others, and builds a legacy of positive impact through consistent generosity."
>
> *Must Action example:* Volunteer or mentor someone for 2 hours monthly.

The Wheel Must Roll Smoothly

Imagine the Must Circle of Life as a wheel with seven spokes. Each spoke represents one of the domains above.

Now imagine trying to roll a wheel with one broken spoke. It doesn't matter how strong the other six spokes are—the wheel will wobble. You might make progress, but the ride will be rough, inefficient, and unsustainable.

This is what happens when you neglect an entire life domain. You might achieve tremendous success in your career, but if your health is failing or your relationships are crumbling, that success feels hollow and temporary.

As Zig Ziglar emphasized: "You can't truly be considered successful in your business life if your home life is in shambles."

True success requires balance across all domains.

EXAMPLE: The Wobbly Wheel

> *Michael was a successful attorney. Career: 9/10. Finances: 9/10. Everything else: 3/10 or below.*
>
> *At 42, he had a heart attack. Not severe, but a wake-up call. The doctor's words haunted him: "Your career won't matter if you're dead."*

Michael realized his wheel was broken. No exercise. Poor diet. No spiritual practice. Strained marriage. Zero community involvement.

He didn't quit his job. He just started strengthening the other spokes. One habit at a time. Health first. Then relationships. Then spiritual practice.

Two years later, his career was still strong (8/10—he learned he didn't need perfect). But now Health was 7/10. Relationships 8/10. Spiritual 6/10. The wheel rolled smoothly.

THE MUST CIRCLE OF LIFE ASSESSMENT

Finding Your Starting Point

The key to using the Must Circle of Life effectively is knowing where to start. You can't fix everything at once, so you need to identify which spoke needs the most attention.

Take a moment to honestly assess where you are in each domain. Rate yourself on a scale of 1-10:

- 1-3: This area is critically neglected and causing real problems
- 4-6: You're functional but not thriving—this area needs attention
- 7-8: You're doing well and maintaining good habits
- 9-10: This area is flourishing

Complete this assessment now:

Life Domain	Current Rating (1-10)	Key Question to Consider
Health & Vitality		Do I have energy? Am I taking care of my body?
Relationships & Love		Are my closest relationships thriving?
Career & Professional		Am I growing and contributing in my work?
Financial Well-Being		Am I building security and freedom?
Personal Growth		Am I learning and expanding?
Spiritual & Peace of Mind		Do I have inner peace and spiritual practice?
Community & Legacy		Am I contributing beyond myself?

Be brutally honest with yourself. Self-deception here will sabotage everything that follows.

Start With Your Weakest Spoke

Once you've identified your weakest spoke, that's where you begin building habits. Not because it's easy, but because it will have the greatest impact on your overall well-being.

If Health & Vitality is your lowest score, start there. Create your I AM Statement for that domain. Design one Must Action. Build that habit until it's automatic.

If Relationships & Love is struggling, focus there first. Everything else can wait.

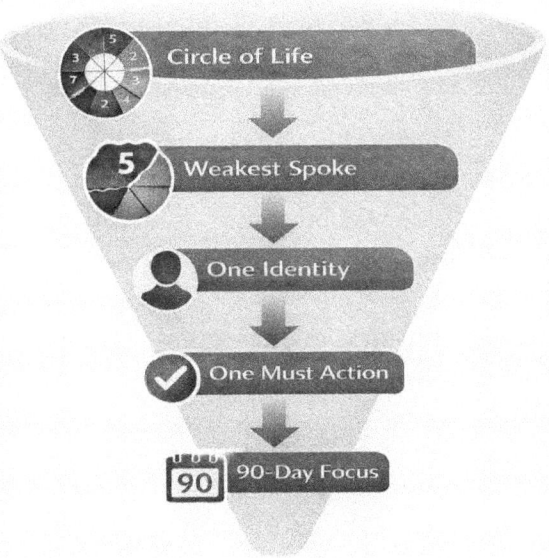

How to Choose Your First Must Habit

- Circle of Life
- Weakest Spoke
- One Identity
- One Must Action
- 90-Day Focus

This focused approach might feel counterintuitive—especially if you're tempted to work on your strengths. But strengthening what's already strong doesn't fix the wheel. You need to repair the broken spoke.

The Balance Principle: Progress, Not Perfection

Here's what balance does NOT mean:

- Spending equal time in every domain (impossible and undesirable)
- Being a 10/10 in every area simultaneously (unrealistic)
- Never prioritizing one area over another (sometimes you must)

Balance DOES mean:

- No domain is completely neglected
- You're making consistent progress in your weakest areas
- You have at least one Must Action in each critical domain
- When you temporarily focus on one area, you maintain minimum viable habits in the others

Success in one area does not compensate for failure in another.

Seasonal Prioritization Within the Circle

Life has seasons. There will be times when you must temporarily prioritize one domain:

- Launching a business might require intense focus on Career for 6-12 months
- Recovering from illness might demand prioritizing Health & Vitality
- A new baby requires heavy investment in Relationships & Love

This is not imbalance. This is strategic focus.

But here's the key: even during seasons of intense focus, you must maintain minimum viable habits in the other domains.

If you're launching a business, you still move your body for 15 minutes daily (Health). You still have one quality conversation with your partner (Relationships). You still meditate for 5 minutes each morning (Spiritual).

These minimum viable habits keep the other spokes from breaking entirely while you focus on one area intensely.

Building One Spoke at a Time

The temptation is to try fixing all seven domains simultaneously. Resist it.

Focus on one domain. Build one habit. Give it time to become automatic.

Once that habit is solid (at least 66-90 days), move to your next weakest spoke and repeat.

This sequential approach feels slow, but it's sustainable. Trying to build seven habits at once is a recipe for overwhelm and failure.

Over the course of a year, you can strengthen all seven spokes. That's transformative.

> **THE NEUROSCIENCE: Why Multitasking New Habits Fails**
>
> *Your prefrontal cortex—the brain region responsible for self-control and decision-making—has limited bandwidth. When you try to build multiple new habits simultaneously, you overload this system.*
>
> *Research by Stanford behavior scientist BJ Fogg shows that people who try to change multiple behaviors at once have a 90% failure rate. But people who focus on one tiny habit at a time have a 70-80% success rate. Your brain simply cannot encode multiple new neural pathways simultaneously. Sequential habit-building works because it allows one pathway to solidify before you begin constructing the next.*

What's Coming in Chapter 4

You now have:

- Your I Am Statement (Identity)
- Your Chosen Domain (Where To Focus)
- Your Understanding Of Balance (The Big Picture)

But how do you actually execute your Must Action consistently? How do you translate identity into daily proof? How do you live in the Must Zone—that dynamic state where your actions flow naturally from who you are?

That's what Chapter 4 is about.

A wheel with seven strong spokes rolls smoothly.

A wheel with one broken spoke wobbles.

Build your habits strategically. Strengthen every spoke.

PART II
THE SCIENCE

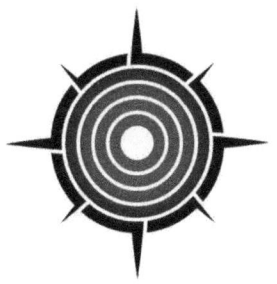

CHAPTER 4

Living in the Must Zone

The Must Zone is a dynamic, purpose-driven state where your actions are fueled by commitment to your core values, transcending the limitations of the comfort zone.
— From Must: Becoming the Person You Are Meant to Be

Thomas knew what he needed to do.

For three years, he'd been saying "I am a writer." He had the I AM Statement. He had the Must Purpose. He even had a detailed plan: write 500 words every morning before work.

He just... didn't do it.

Most mornings, he'd hit snooze. Or he'd make coffee and "just check email real quick." Or he'd sit down to write, stare at the blank page, and convince himself he needed more preparation.

The problem wasn't the goal. It wasn't the identity. It was the gap between knowing and doing.

Thomas knew WHO he was. He just hadn't built the system to PROVE it daily.

Then he learned about Must Actions and the Must Zone.

Instead of vague intentions ("write in the morning"), he created a precise Must Action: "Right after I pour my coffee, I open my laptop, think 'I am a writer,' and write one sentence."

Not 500 words. One sentence.

The shift was immediate. One sentence was so small he couldn't refuse. And once he wrote one sentence, he usually wrote fifty. But even when he didn't—even when it was truly just one sentence—he'd proven his identity.

Six months later, Thomas had written 73,000 words. Not because he felt motivated every day. Because his Must Action was so small, so specific, and so aligned with his identity that it became automatic.

He wasn't trying to write anymore. He was living in the Must Zone.

The Gap Between Identity and Action

You've identified your I AM Statement. You've chosen a domain from the Must Circle of Life. You know what you need to do.

But here's where most people fail: they know who they want to be, but they don't consistently DO what that identity requires.

The gap between identity and action is where transformation dies.

This chapter is about closing that gap permanently. It's about translating your I AM Statement into Must Actions—the daily, nonnegotiable behaviors that prove you are who you say you are.

And it's about living in the Must Zone—the dynamic state where your actions are so aligned with your identity that resistance disappears and flow becomes your default.

What Are Must Actions?

Must Actions are the deliberate, focused behaviors that drive you forward, even when challenges arise. They are the nonnegotiable steps you must take to align your life with your deepest aspirations, Must Values, and Must Standards.

Must Actions are not suggestions. They are not preferences. They are identity requirements.

If you declare "I am a writer," then writing daily is a Must Action. If you declare "I am someone who honors my body," then moving daily is a Must Action. If you declare "I am a present parent," then putting your phone away during family time is a Must Action.

Must Actions are the bridge between who you say you are and who you actually are. They are the proof of your identity.

The Four Criteria of Effective Must Actions

Not every action qualifies as a Must Action. To be truly effective, your Must Actions must meet four criteria:

1. Aligned with Your I AM Statement

Every Must Action must flow directly from your declared identity.

If your I AM Statement is "I am someone who values deep relationships," then a Must Action might be having one meaningful conversation daily with someone you care about.

If your I AM Statement is "I am financially disciplined," then a Must Action might be tracking every expense and reviewing your budget weekly.

The action must serve the identity. If there's no clear connection, it's not a Must Action—it's just a task.

2. Observable and Concrete

Must Actions must be specific behaviors you can verify.

"Be healthier" is NOT a Must Action. It's a vague intention.

"Walk for 30 minutes every morning" IS a Must Action. It's binary: you either did it or you didn't.

Vague goals create ambiguity. Ambiguity creates excuses. Must Actions eliminate both.

3. Small Enough to Do Daily

Must Actions must be sustainable. If the behavior is too large or complex, you won't maintain it.

"Write a book" is NOT a Must Action. It's overwhelming and abstract.

"Write 500 words every morning" IS a Must Action. It's achievable, repeatable, and compounds over time.

Start with the smallest version that still counts as proof of your identity.

4. Creates Immediate Feedback

Must Actions should provide instant evidence that you're living your identity.

Every time you complete a Must Action, you get a small win. That win reinforces the identity. The identity makes the next Must Action easier.

This creates a positive feedback loop: action proves identity → identity drives action → action proves identity.

Must Actions Across the Must Circle of Life

Here are specific Must Actions for each domain:

Health & Vitality

- Move your body for 30 minutes (walk, yoga, strength training)
- Drink 64 oz of water daily
- Get 7-8 hours of sleep by maintaining a consistent bedtime
- Eat a protein-rich breakfast within 1 hour of waking

Relationships & Love

- Have one distraction-free conversation with your partner daily
- Send a thoughtful text to a friend or family member
- Put your phone away during dinner
- Schedule one quality time activity weekly with someone you love

Career & Professional Development

- Complete your most important task before checking email
- Spend 30 minutes on skill development daily
- Review your top 3 priorities each morning
- Send one networking or relationship-building message daily

Financial Well-Being

- Track every expense daily
- Automate savings transfers on payday
- Review your budget weekly
- Have no-spend days twice per week

Personal Growth & Learning

- Read or listen to educational content for 20 minutes daily
- Journal for 10 minutes about what you learned
- Practice a new skill for 15 minutes
- Take an online course or watch educational videos

Spiritual and Peace of Mind

- Meditate for 10 minutes each morning
- Practice gratitude journaling (3 things daily)
- Pray or engage in spiritual reading
- Spend time in nature weekly

Community & Legacy

- Volunteer 2 hours monthly
- Mentor one person consistently
- Perform one act of service weekly
- Contribute to causes you care about

Understanding the Must Zone

The Must Zone is where magic happens. It's the state where your actions flow naturally from your identity, where resistance disappears, and where showing up feels as automatic as breathing.

Most people live in one of three zones:

The Comfort Zone: This is where everything feels safe and familiar. No growth happens here. You're coasting, not climbing.

The Panic Zone: This is where everything feels overwhelming. You're trying to change too much, too fast. Burnout lives here.

The Must Zone: This is the sweet spot between comfort and panic. You're challenged but not overwhelmed. Growth is happening, but it feels aligned, not forced.

The Three Zones

Characteristics of the Must Zone

You know you're in the Must Zone when:

- Your Must Actions feel challenging but achievable
- You show up consistently without massive willpower
- You experience flow states more frequently
- Resistance is present but manageable
- You feel aligned with your values and purpose
- Growth feels natural, not forced

Comparing Your Zones

Zone	Feels Like	Result
Comfort Zone	Safe, familiar	Stagnation
Panic Zone	Overwhelming	Burnout
Must Zone	Challenging + aligned	Sustainable growth

The Must Zone is sustainable. You can live here indefinitely because your actions are rooted in identity, not dependent on motivation.

EXAMPLE: From Panic to Must

> Sophia wanted to get healthy. She committed to: gym 6x/week, meal prep every Sunday, 10K steps daily, no sugar, meditation 30 min/day, and journaling.
>
> She lasted 11 days. Then she crashed. Total burnout. Panic Zone.
>
> She restarted with ONE Must Action: "Right after I pour my coffee, I put on workout clothes." That's it. No gym requirement. Just clothes.
>
> This was the Must Zone. Challenging (it required getting up earlier), but achievable (2 minutes max). After 30 days, wearing workout clothes felt automatic. Then she added: "After wearing clothes, I walk to the end of my street."
>
> Six months later, Sophia was exercising 5x/week, eating well, and meditating. Not because she forced it all at once. Because she built one Must Action at a time in the Must Zone.

THE NEUROSCIENCE: Why Must Actions Work

When you perform a Must Action, you activate the basal ganglia—the brain region responsible for habit formation. Simultaneously, connecting the action to your identity (via your I AM Statement) engages the medial prefrontal cortex, which processes self-concept.

This dual activation creates what neuroscientists call "identity consolidation"—your brain simultaneously encodes the behavior as automatic AND reinforces it as part of your self-concept. This is why identity-based habits stick better than behavior-based habits: they're being written into two neural systems at once.

How to Enter the Must Zone

Entering the Must Zone requires three steps:

Step 1: Choose ONE Must Action

Not five. Not ten. One.

Look at your weakest spoke in the Must Circle of Life. Choose the single most important behavior that would prove the identity you want to build in that domain.

Make it small enough that you can't refuse it. Make it specific enough that you can verify completion.

Step 2: Connect It to Your Identity

Before you perform the Must Action each day, take three seconds to remind yourself of your I AM Statement.

This mental connection is what keeps you in the Must Zone. You're not forcing yourself to do something you don't want to do. You're proving who you already are.

Step 3: Create Evidence Daily

Track your Must Action every single day. Mark it on a calendar. Write it in a journal. Use a habit app. The specific method doesn't matter.

What matters is creating visible evidence that accumulates. This evidence serves two purposes:

1. It proves to your brain that you ARE the person you claim to be
2. It becomes its own source of motivation (you don't want to break the streak)

Common Mistakes That Keep You Out of the Must Zone

Mistake #1: Starting Too Big

You commit to running 5 miles when you should commit to putting on your running shoes. Ambition kills habits in the early stages.

Solution: Make your Must Action embarrassingly small. If it takes more than 2 minutes, it's too big.

Mistake #2: Trying to Build Multiple Habits Simultaneously

You attempt to fix Health, Relationships, Career, and Spiritual all at once. Within two weeks, you're overwhelmed.

Solution: Build one habit to automaticity (66-90 days), then add the next.

Mistake #3: Forgetting the Identity Connection

You perform the action mechanically without connecting it to your I AM Statement.

Solution: Take 3 seconds before each Must Action to remind yourself: "I am someone who..."

Mistake #4: No Visible Evidence

You perform the habit but don't track it. Without evidence, your brain doesn't encode proof.

Solution: Mark it on a calendar. Every. Single. Day.

TOOL: The Must Action Builder

Use this template to design your first Must Action:

My weakest spoke (from Chapter 3 assessment):

_____

My I AM Statement for this domain:

_____

_____

The ONE behavior that would prove this identity:

_____

My Must Action (make it tiny, specific, daily):

_____

How I will track this daily:

_____

My 90-day commitment start date:

_____

Your First Week in the Must Zone

The first week is critical. Here's what to expect:

- Day 1-2: High motivation. The Must Action feels exciting. This is the honeymoon.
- Day 3-4: Novelty fades slightly. The Must Action requires more conscious effort. This is normal.
- Day 5-7: First test of commitment. You might miss a day. If you do, restart immediately. Don't spiral.

Remember: You're building a neural pathway. It takes repetition. The first week proves willingness. The next 60 days prove commitment.

What's Coming in Chapter 5

You now understand:

- What Must Actions are (identity requirements)
- The four criteria they must meet
- How to enter the Must Zone
- Common mistakes to avoid

But how do you design the perfect habit loop? How do you create a system that makes your Must Action automatic?

Chapter 5 reveals the Must Habit Loop—the exact 4-step framework your brain uses to encode behaviors into automaticity.

Identity without action is fantasy.

Action without identity is exhausting.

Identity + Action = The Must Zone.

CHAPTER 5

The Must Habit Loop— How Change Happens

We are what we repeatedly do.
Excellence, then, is not an act, but a habit.
— Aristotle (via Will Durant)

Lisa had tried to meditate for five years.

She bought apps. Read books. Attended workshops. Joined challenges. Each attempt followed the same pattern: excited start, gradual decline, eventual abandonment.

The problem wasn't commitment. It was chaos.

She had no system. Some mornings she'd meditate after coffee. Other days before breakfast. Sometimes in her bedroom, sometimes on the couch. The time varied. The location shifted. The duration fluctuated.

There was no loop. Just random attempts powered by willpower.

Then Lisa learned about the Must Habit Loop—a precise 4-step framework that her brain could actually encode.

She redesigned everything:

- Signal: Right after I pour my morning coffee
- Identity: I think "I am someone who cultivates inner peace"
- Tiny Action: Sit on my meditation cushion for 60 seconds
- Evidence + Celebration: Mark X on calendar, say "I honored my peace today"

Same time. Same location. Same sequence. Same celebration. Every single day.

Ninety days later, meditation was automatic. Not because she finally had enough willpower. Because she gave her brain a loop it could encode.

Why Most Habit Advice Fails

Most habit advice focuses on motivation. "Get excited!" "Stay committed!" "Don't give up!"

But motivation is unreliable. It surges and crashes. It depends on mood, energy, circumstances.

Your brain doesn't run on motivation. It runs on loops.

A habit is simply a behavior that your brain has encoded into an automatic loop. When the loop is complete, the behavior runs without conscious effort.

The Must Habit Loop gives your brain exactly what it needs to encode automaticity: a clear signal, a strong identity connection, a tiny action, and immediate evidence.

The Must Habit Loop: Four Steps to Automaticity

The Must Habit Loop has four components. Each is essential. Skip one, and the loop breaks.

The Must Habit Loop

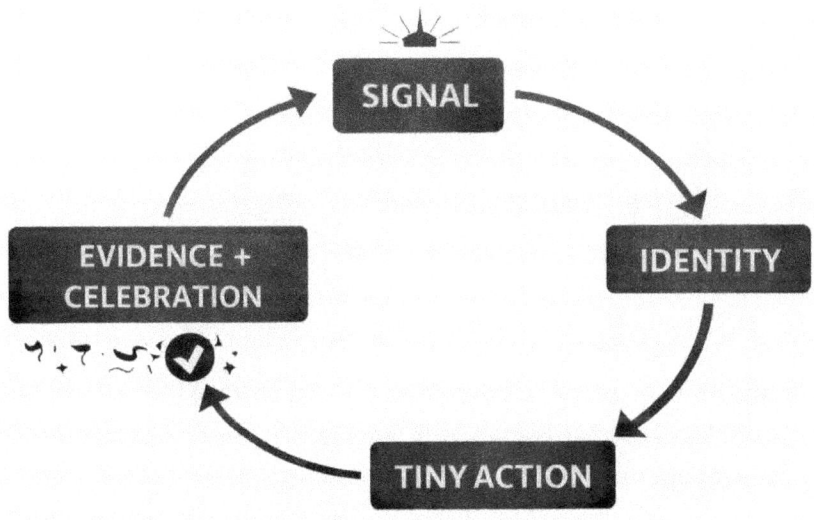

STEP 1: THE SIGNAL

The signal is the trigger that initiates your habit. It tells your brain: "It's time to execute this behavior."

The best signals are:

- Already happening in your routine (existing behaviors)
- Highly specific (precise time or action, not vague)
- Consistent (happens every day at roughly the same time)

Examples of effective signals:

- "Right after I pour my morning coffee..."
- "When my alarm goes off at 6:00 AM..."
- "As soon as I sit down at my desk..."
- "Right after I brush my teeth..."

Examples of WEAK signals:

- "In the morning" (too vague)
- "When I have time" (never happens)
- "When I feel motivated" (unreliable)

The key is specificity. Your brain needs precision. "After I pour my coffee" is infinitely better than "sometime in the morning."

The Power of Habit Stacking

The most effective signals are existing behaviors. This technique is called habit stacking: you anchor your new habit to something you already do automatically.

Formula: "After I [EXISTING HABIT], I will [NEW HABIT]."

Examples:

- After I pour my coffee, I will sit on my meditation cushion
- After I brush my teeth, I will do 5 pushups
- After I close my laptop for the day, I will write in my gratitude journal
- After I get in bed, I will read one page

The existing habit becomes the automatic trigger. You don't need to remember. Your brain already knows the sequence.

STEP 2: THE IDENTITY REMINDER

This is what makes the Must Habit Loop different from generic habit advice. Between the signal and the action, you pause for three seconds to remind yourself of your I AM Statement.

Why this matters:

Without the identity reminder, you're just forcing yourself to do something. You're relying on willpower. You're building a behavior-based habit.

With the identity reminder, you're proving who you are. You're aligning action with identity. You're building an identity-based habit.

The three-second pause changes everything.

Examples:

- Signal: After I pour my coffee → Identity: "I am someone who cultivates peace" → Action: Sit on cushion
- Signal: When my alarm goes off → Identity: "I am someone who honors my body" → Action: Put on workout clothes
- Signal: When I open my laptop → Identity: "I am a writer" → Action: Write one sentence

STEP 3: THE TINY ACTION

This is the behavior itself—but made absurdly small.

The 2-Minute Rule: Your tiny action should take less than 2 minutes to complete.

Why so small? Because small actions eliminate resistance. You can't refuse something that takes 60 seconds.

Examples of tiny actions:

- "Sit on my meditation cushion for 60 seconds" (not "meditate for 20 minutes")
- "Put on my workout clothes" (not "complete a full workout")
- "Write one sentence" (not "write 1000 words")
- "Read one page" (not "read for an hour")
- "Track today's expenses" (not "create a complete budget")

But won't I stay stuck doing tiny actions?

No. Here's what happens:

Most days, once you start the tiny action, momentum takes over. You sit on the cushion for 60 seconds and end up meditating for 10 minutes. You put on workout clothes and end up exercising.

But even on days when you only do the tiny action—even when it's truly just 60 seconds or one sentence—you still proved your identity. You still cast a vote for who you're becoming.

The habit is showing up, not intensity.

EXAMPLE: The Power of Tiny Actions

> *Rebecca wanted to write a book. She committed to "write 2000 words daily." Lasted 4 days. Too big.*
>
> *She restarted with "write one sentence daily after coffee." For the first week, most days were literally one sentence. Then two. Then a paragraph.*
>
> *Six months later: 62,000 words written. Not because she forced 2000 words daily. Because she showed up for one sentence daily and momentum did the rest.*

STEP 4: EVIDENCE + CELEBRATION

Every time you complete your tiny action, you create evidence that you are who you say you are.

This evidence is critical. It strengthens the neural pathway connecting the signal to the action. It reinforces your I AM Statement. It makes the next repetition easier.

But evidence alone isn't enough. You need to celebrate.

Celebration triggers dopamine—the neurotransmitter that tells your brain "this behavior is worth repeating." Without celebration, the habit loop is incomplete.

How to celebrate:

- Fist pump
- Say "Yes!" or "I did it!"
- Take a deep breath and smile
- Check a box on your tracker
- Text an accountability partner
- Say your I AM Statement out loud ("I'm a writer!")

The key is immediacy. Celebrate within seconds of completing the action. This creates a tight feedback loop that tells your brain: "This behavior feels good. Do it again tomorrow."

Don't skip the celebration because it feels silly. Your brain doesn't care if the celebration is proportionate to the action. It only cares that the dopamine hit happens.

THE NEUROSCIENCE: The Dopamine-Driven Loop

When you celebrate immediately after completing a habit, your brain releases dopamine. This dopamine spike creates a pleasure-reward association with the behavior.

Research by Wolfram Schultz at Cambridge shows that dopamine isn't just about pleasure—it's about learning. The dopamine signal tells your brain: "Remember this sequence. Repeat it tomorrow." Over time, the brain begins anticipating the dopamine hit, which makes the habit feel intrinsically rewarding even before you complete it. This is why celebrating—however small—is non-negotiable for habit formation.

The Complete Loop in Action

Let's see how all four steps work together in practice.

EXAMPLE 1: Building a Daily Writing Habit

- Signal: Right after I pour my morning coffee
- Identity: I think to myself: "I am a writer"
- Tiny Action: Write one sentence in my journal
- Evidence + Celebration: Check the box on my habit tracker and say "I'm a writer" out loud

Notice the specificity. The signal isn't "in the morning"—it's "right after I pour my coffee." The tiny action isn't "write a lot"—it's "one sentence." The celebration is immediate and reinforces the identity.

EXAMPLE 2: Building a Daily Movement Habit

- Signal: When my alarm goes off at 6:00 AM
- Identity: I remind myself: "I am someone who honors my body through movement"
- Tiny Action: Put on my workout clothes
- Evidence + Celebration: Mark an X on my calendar and say "I honored my body today"

Notice: Once you're in workout clothes, you almost always exercise. But even if you don't, you still proved your identity. The habit is showing up, not intensity.

EXAMPLE 3: Building a Financial Tracking Habit

- Signal: Right before I get in bed
- Identity: "I am financially disciplined."
- Tiny Action: Log today's expenses in my app (takes 90 seconds)

- Evidence + Celebration: Watch my streak counter increase, say "I'm building wealth"

Designing Your Must Habit Loop

Now it's time to design your own loop. Take the Must Action you identified in Chapter 4 and build a complete habit loop around it.

Step 1: Choose Your Signal

Pick a signal that is:

- Already happening in your routine (an existing behavior or time)
- Highly specific (precise time or action, not vague)
- Consistent (happens every day at roughly the same time)

The easiest signals are existing behaviors. "After I pour my coffee" is easier than "7:30 AM" because you pour coffee every day naturally.

Step 2: Connect to Your Identity

Your I AM Statement should already be clear from Chapter 2. When the signal appears, take three seconds to remind yourself of that identity.

This mental reminder shifts your motivation from external ("I should do this") to internal ("This is who I am").

Step 3: Define Your Tiny Action

Make your Must Action as small as possible while still counting as proof of your identity.

Ask yourself: "What's the smallest version of this behavior that still proves I'm the person I say I am?"

The tiny action should take less than 2 minutes.

Step 4: Plan Your Evidence and Celebration

Decide in advance how you'll track and celebrate.

Evidence could be:

- A checkmark on a wall calendar
- A note in your journal
- A mark in a habit tracking app
- A photo of yourself doing the habit

Celebration should be:

- Immediate (within 10 seconds of finishing)
- Genuine (something that actually makes you feel good)
- Consistent (the same celebration each time)

Common Mistakes That Break the Loop

Mistake #1: Vague Signals

"I'll do it in the morning" is not a signal. It's a wish. Your brain needs precision.

Vague: "I'll meditate in the morning"

Specific: "Right after I brush my teeth, I'll sit on my meditation cushion"

Mistake #2: Starting Too Big

Ambition kills habits. You get excited about transformation and commit to running 5 miles daily when you should commit to putting on your running shoes.

Solution: Start absurdly small. Once the habit is automatic (after 66+ days), you can increase intensity.

Mistake #3: Skipping the Identity Reminder

Many people jump straight from signal to action. They skip the identity component.

This works for behavior-based habits. But it doesn't work for identity-based habits. The three-second identity reminder is what transforms a behavior into proof.

Mistake #4: Forgetting to Celebrate

This is the most common mistake. People complete the action but don't celebrate because it feels trivial.

Without celebration, you're not encoding the habit. You're just forcing yourself to do something. The celebration is what tells your brain to repeat the behavior tomorrow.

Mistake #5: Inconsistent Execution

The loop only works if you repeat it consistently. Missing one day isn't fatal. But missing three days in a row breaks the pattern.

Your brain needs repetition to encode automaticity. Sporadic execution means the behavior never becomes automatic.

TOOL: The Habit Loop Builder

Use this template to design your Must Habit Loop:

MY MUST HABIT LOOP

1. THE SIGNAL (What triggers this habit?)

After I _____

When _____

Right before I _____

2. THE IDENTITY REMINDER (What will I think?)

"I am someone who _____

3. THE TINY ACTION (What will I do? Make it <2 minutes)

I will _____

4. THE EVIDENCE + CELEBRATION (How will I track and celebrate?)

Track: _____

Celebrate: _____

My 66-day commitment starts:

_____

What's Coming in Chapter 6

You now have the complete Must Habit Loop—the precise 4-step framework your brain uses to encode behaviors into automaticity.

But you still have critical questions:

- How long does this actually take?
- What happens during the formation process?
- Why do some habits feel automatic in weeks while others take months?

Chapter 6 reveals the truth about habit formation timelines. We'll debunk the myths (21 days, 30 days) and show you what the science actually says.

A habit without a loop is random.

A loop without consistency is wishful thinking.

A complete loop, repeated daily, becomes automatic.

CHAPTER 6

The Truth About 66 Days

Patience is bitter, but its fruit is sweet.
— Aristotle

Kevin quit on day 22.

He'd read that it takes 21 days to form a habit. So he committed to daily exercise for three weeks. Push through 21 days, and it becomes automatic. That's what the internet promised.

On day 22, he woke up expecting the habit to feel easy. Natural. Automatic.

It didn't.

Exercise still required effort. He still had to convince himself to go to the gym. Nothing felt automatic.

Kevin concluded something was wrong with him. If 21 days was enough for everyone else, why wasn't it enough for him?

So he quit.

The truth? There was nothing wrong with Kevin. There was something wrong with the 21-day myth.

Exercise is a complex habit. It doesn't become automatic in 21 days. For most people, it takes 60-90 days minimum. Kevin quit right before the breakthrough.

Three years later, Kevin discovered the real science. He committed to 90 days. On day 66, exercise started feeling automatic. By day 90, it was effortless.

The habit was the same. The timeline was different. And that changed everything.

The 21-Day Myth: Where It Came From (And Why It's Wrong)

How long does it take to build a habit?

If you've spent any time in the personal development world, you've probably heard the answer: 21 days. Maybe 30 days if the source is being generous.

These numbers are everywhere. Books, articles, coaches, apps—they all promise that if you just stick with something for three weeks or a month, it will become automatic.

There's only one problem: it's not true.

The 21-day myth is one of the most persistent and damaging pieces of misinformation in habit science. And the 30-day version isn't much better. Both set unrealistic expectations that set people up for failure.

Where the Myth Came From

The 21-day myth originated with Dr. Maxwell Maltz, a plastic surgeon in the 1960s.

Dr. Maltz noticed that his patients seemed to take about 21 days to get used to their new faces after surgery. He also observed that it took him about 21 days to form a new habit himself.

He published these observations in his book Psycho-Cybernetics.

But here's the critical detail everyone forgets: Maltz said it took "a minimum of about 21 days" for people to adjust to change.

Minimum. Not average. Not guaranteed. And his observations were anecdotal, not based on controlled research.

Somehow, over decades of repetition, "a minimum of about 21 days" became "exactly 21 days to form any habit." The nuance disappeared. The myth was born.

The Real Science: What Research Actually Shows

So if it's not 21 days, how long does it actually take?

The most rigorous research on this question comes from Dr. Phillippa Lally and her team at University College London. Their study, published in the European Journal of Social Psychology, tracked 96 people as they built new habits over an extended period.

The results were revealing:

The average time to reach automaticity was 66 days.

But that average hides significant variation. Depending on the habit and the person, it took anywhere from 18 days to 254 days for a behavior to become automatic.

Let that sink in. The range is enormous. Some simple habits clicked into place in less than three weeks. Some complex habits took more than eight months.

Habit Formation Timeline

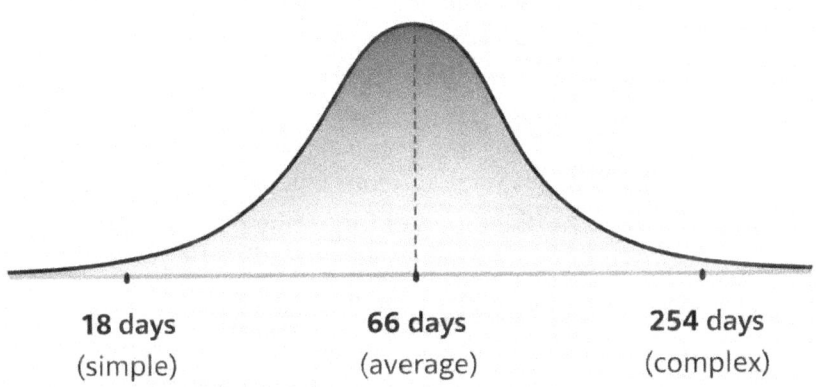

18 days (simple)   **66 days** (average)   **254 days** (complex)

What Determines How Long Your Habit Takes

Why such a wide range? The research identified several factors that affect habit formation speed:

1. Complexity of the Behavior

Simple behaviors become automatic faster. Drinking a glass of water with lunch can become habitual in as little as 18-20 days. Taking a vitamin with breakfast follows a similar timeline.

Complex behaviors take much longer. Exercise is particularly difficult. A 2015 study found that people needed to work out at least four times per week for a minimum of six weeks before exercise began to feel habitual. And even then, many people needed significantly more time.

Writing, meditation, learning a new skill—these complex habits often take 90-120 days or more to feel truly automatic.

2. Consistency of Execution

The more consistently you perform the behavior, the faster it becomes automatic.

Missing a day here and there slows the process. Missing several days in a row can reset progress significantly.

This is why having a clear signal (from Chapter 5) is so important. The signal reduces the likelihood of forgetting or skipping.

3. Strength of the Identity Connection

This is where the Must framework gives you an advantage.

When a habit is deeply connected to your I AM Statement, it encodes faster because you're not just building a behavior—you're reinforcing an identity.

Someone who identifies as "a person who values health" will build exercise habits faster than someone who just "wants to lose weight." The identity provides intrinsic motivation that speeds up the encoding process.

4. Environmental Support

Habits that fit easily into your existing environment and routine form faster than habits that require significant environmental changes.

If you want to meditate but have to rearrange your entire morning, it will take longer. If you can meditate right after an existing routine (like making coffee), it will encode faster.

> **THE NEUROSCIENCE: What's Happening in Your Brain**
>
> *When you repeat a behavior consistently, your brain begins forming a neural pathway in the basal ganglia—the region responsible for habit formation. Each*

repetition strengthens this pathway through a process called myelination, where the neural connections become coated with myelin (a fatty substance that speeds signal transmission).

Think of it like carving a path through a forest. The first time, you're hacking through dense brush. The second time, it's slightly easier. By the 50th time, there's a clear trail. By day 66, the path is so well-worn that your feet follow it automatically. This is why consistency matters: each repetition deepens the groove.

The Three Phases of Habit Formation

Understanding the timeline is important, but understanding the phases is even more critical. Every habit goes through three distinct phases on its journey to automaticity:

The Three Phases of Habit Formation

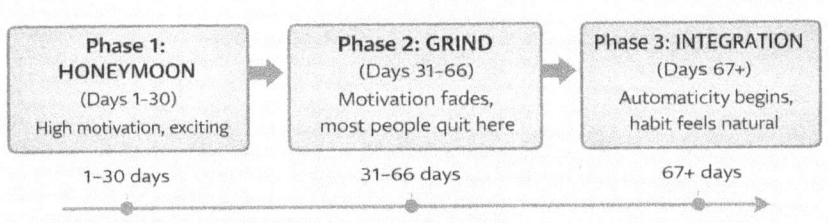

PHASE 1: THE HONEYMOON (Days 1-30)

This is the easy phase. You're motivated. You're excited. The habit is new and interesting. Completing it feels like progress.

But don't mistake this phase for success. You're not even halfway to automaticity yet.

At 30 days, the habit still requires conscious effort. You still need willpower. You still have to remind yourself to do it.

Many people quit around day 25-30 because they expect the habit to feel automatic by now. It doesn't. And they interpret that as failure.

It's not failure. It's normal. Thirty days is just the beginning.

PHASE 2: THE GRIND (Days 31-66)

This is where most habits die.

The novelty has worn off. The initial motivation has faded. The habit doesn't feel easier yet. And you start questioning whether it's worth it.

This is the phase where your identity becomes critical. You have to lean on your I AM Statement. You have to remind yourself that you're not doing this to achieve a goal—you're doing this because it's who you are.

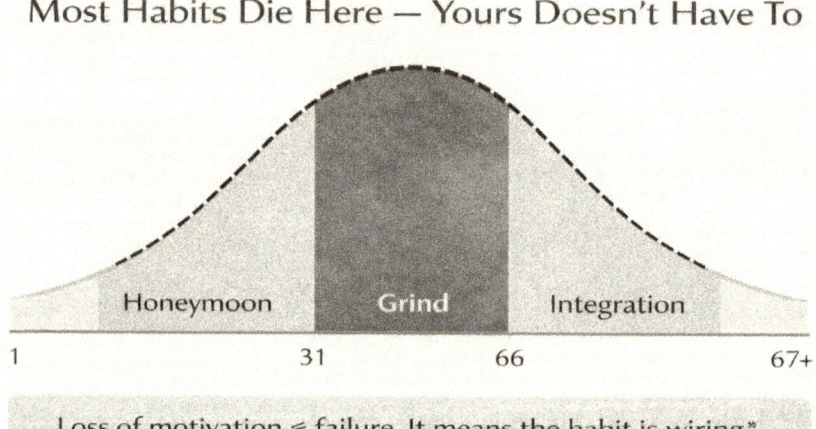

Loss of motivation ≠ failure. It means the habit is wiring."

This phase is where the real encoding happens. Your brain is building the neural pathways that will eventually make the behavior automatic. But that process is invisible. You can't feel it happening.

The only way through Phase 2 is consistency. Show up every day. Execute the tiny action. Celebrate the evidence. Trust the process.

EXAMPLE: Surviving the Grind

Amanda was meditating daily. Days 1-30 felt great. Days 31-50 felt terrible. She questioned everything: "Is this even working? Should I try a different technique? Maybe I'm not cut out for meditation."

She didn't quit. She kept showing up. On day 58, something shifted. Meditation felt slightly easier. By day 66, she stopped thinking about whether to meditate. She just did it.

The Grind wasn't proof that meditation didn't work. It was proof that her brain was rewiring.

PHASE 3: INTEGRATION (Days 67+)

This is where the magic happens.

Somewhere around day 66 (give or take a few weeks depending on the habit), the behavior starts to feel automatic.

You stop thinking about it consciously. You just do it. The signal appears, and the behavior follows without deliberation.

This is true automaticity. This is what you've been working toward.

But even in Phase 3, you're not done. The habit needs to be maintained. If you stop doing it for several weeks, the automation can fade. The neural pathway weakens.

This is why habits need to be lifetime practices, not short-term projects. Once you reach Phase 3, the habit requires almost no effort to maintain—but it still requires consistency.

What to Expect During the First 90 Days

Here's a realistic timeline for what habit formation actually looks like:

Days 1-7: The Excitement

Motivation is high. The habit feels new and interesting. Completion rates are usually high. This is the easiest week.

Days 8-21: The First Test

The novelty starts to fade. You miss a day or two. You start to feel resistance. This is normal. The key is getting back on track immediately.

Days 22-30: The False Summit

Many people expect to feel automatic by now. You won't. The habit still requires effort. Don't interpret this as failure. You're only a third of the way there.

Days 31-50: The Grind Intensifies

This is the hardest stretch. Motivation is gone. The habit doesn't feel easier. Many people quit here. Don't. This is where you build the foundation.

Days 51-66: The Shift Begins

You start to notice small shifts. The habit feels slightly easier. You forget to do it less often. You're approaching automaticity.

Days 67-90: Integration

The habit starts to feel natural. You do it without thinking. True automaticity has begun. But you still need to maintain it.

Why People Quit (And How to Avoid It)

Most people quit habits because they believe the myth. They think 21 or 30 days should be enough. When the habit still feels hard at day 25, they conclude something is wrong.

Nothing is wrong. They're just early.

Here's how to avoid this trap:

1. Set the right expectation from the start

Know that you're committing to at least 66 days. Ideally 90. This isn't discouraging—it's realistic.

2. Focus on the process, not the outcome

Don't ask "Is this automatic yet?" Ask "Did I show up today?" The only metric that matters is consistency.

3. Use your identity as fuel

When motivation fades (and it will), lean on your I AM Statement. You're not doing this to achieve something. You're doing this because it's who you are.

4. Track your evidence ruthlessly

Every day you complete the habit, mark it. Create a visual record. The evidence accumulates and becomes its own source of motivation.

The 90-Day Commitment

Based on the research and experience coaching thousands of people, here's the recommendation:

Commit to 90 days.

Not 21. Not 30. Ninety.

Ninety days is long enough for even complex habits to begin feeling automatic. It's long enough to get through Phase 2—the grind—and into Phase 3—integration.

More importantly, 90 days gives you enough repetitions that the behavior becomes part of your identity, not just a thing you do.

After 90 days of writing every morning, you're not someone trying to become a writer. You're a writer. The identity is proven. The habit is encoded.

TOOL: The 90-Day Tracker

Use this tracker to maintain consistency:

Print a blank calendar or create a spreadsheet with 90 boxes.

Each day you complete your Must Action, mark it:

- ✓ if you completed the full action
- ½ if you completed the tiny version only
- X if you missed the day completely

Your goal: No more than 2 consecutive X marks. Miss two days in a row, and you risk breaking the pattern.

The visual evidence is powerful. When you see 50 checkmarks in a row, breaking the streak feels painful. That pain is motivation.

What's Coming in Part III

You now have the complete system:

- Your I AM Statement defines who you are (Chapter 2)
- The Must Circle of Life shows you where to focus (Chapter 3)
- Must Actions bridge identity and behavior (Chapter 4)
- The Must Habit Loop shows you how to design habits (Chapter 5)
- The 66-day timeline sets realistic expectations (Chapter 6)

Part III gives you ready-to-implement habit templates for each domain of the Must Circle of Life. These are proven Must Habits you can start building immediately.

But remember: choose ONE domain. Build ONE habit. Give it 90 days. Then move to the next.

That's how you build a life that thrives in every dimension.

21 days is a myth.

30 days is incomplete.

66 days is average.

90 days is a safe bet.

And a lifetime is the goal.

PART III
THE TEMPLATES

CHAPTER 7

Health, Relationships & Career Habits

The secret of getting ahead is getting started.
— *Mark Twain*

James completed the Circle of Life assessment. The results were clear: Health was a 3/10.

He knew what he needed to do. Exercise. Eat better. Sleep more. But knowing and doing are different universes.

For years, he'd tried building health habits. Gym memberships. Meal plans. Fitness apps. Each attempt followed the same pattern: excited start, gradual decline, eventual abandonment.

The problem wasn't commitment. It was decision paralysis.

Which habit should he start with? How should he design it? What if he chose wrong?

Then he discovered the templates.

Instead of creating habits from scratch, he used a proven Must Habit template: Daily Movement. The template gave him everything—the signal, the identity statement, the tiny action, the celebration method.

He didn't have to figure anything out. He just had to execute.

Ninety days later, movement was automatic. Not because he had more willpower than before. Because he stopped inventing and started implementing.

How to Use These Templates

This chapter gives you ready-to-use Must Habit templates for the first three domains of the Must Circle of Life: Health & Vitality, Relationships & Love, and Career & Professional Development.

These aren't generic suggestions. They're specific, proven habits designed using the 4-step loop you learned in Chapter 5.

Each template includes:

- The I AM Statement
- The complete Must Habit Loop (Signal → Identity → Tiny Action → Evidence)
- Why this habit works
- Common obstacles and solutions
- How to scale once it's automatic

Remember the principle from Chapter 3: start with your weakest spoke.

Don't try to build habits in all three domains simultaneously. Choose ONE domain, build ONE habit, commit to 90 days, then move to the next.

HEALTH & VITALITY: Building Your Physical Foundation

Health and vitality are the bedrock of well-being, serving as the foundation upon which all other aspects of life are built.

Without energy, focus, and physical wellness, everything else becomes harder. Career performance suffers when you're exhausted. Relationships strain when you're irritable from poor sleep. Personal growth stalls when you lack vitality.

This is why many people start here—not because health habits are easy, but because the returns compound across every other domain.

Here are five proven Must Habits for Health & Vitality, each with a complete habit loop designed for long-term success.

MUST HABIT #1: DAILY MOVEMENT

THE COMPLETE LOOP:

> **I AM Statement:** "I am someone who honors my body through consistent movement."
>
> **Signal:** Right after I pour my morning coffee
>
> **Identity Reminder:** Take 3 seconds to think: "I am someone who moves my body daily"
>
> **Tiny Action:** Put on my workout clothes OR do 5 pushups OR walk to the end of the driveway
>
> **Evidence + Celebration:** Mark an X on the calendar and say "I honored my body today"

WHY THIS WORKS:

The tiny action removes the biggest obstacle to exercise: getting started. Most people fail at movement habits because they commit to running 5 miles when they should commit to putting on their shoes.

Once you put on workout clothes or do 5 pushups, momentum takes over and you almost always continue. But even if you don't—even if you put them on and take them off—you still proved your identity.

The habit is showing up for your body, not intensity.

COMMON OBSTACLES & SOLUTIONS:

Obstacle: "I don't have time in the morning."

Solution: Make it even smaller. Just touch your workout clothes. Or do 1 pushup. The action takes 10 seconds.

Obstacle: "I'm too tired."

Solution: That's exactly when identity matters most. You don't need energy to put on clothes. Let the action create the energy.

Obstacle: "I don't feel motivated."

Solution: You don't need motivation. You need identity. Motivated people exercise when they feel like it. People with exercise identities exercise whether they feel like it or not.

HOW TO SCALE:

After 66 days, when putting on workout clothes feels automatic, increase the tiny action:

- Week 10-12: Walk to the end of the street
- Week 13-16: Walk around the block
- Week 17+: Complete a full workout routine

But never remove the tiny action as an option. On hard days, you can always fall back to just putting on the clothes. That still counts.

MUST HABIT #2: DAILY HYDRATION

THE COMPLETE LOOP:

> **I AM Statement:** "I am someone who nourishes my body with what it needs."
>
> **Signal:** Every time I sit down at my desk
>
> **Identity Reminder:** "My body deserves proper hydration"

Tiny Action: Drink one full glass of water

Evidence + Celebration: Keep a tally in your journal. Celebrate when you hit 8 glasses.

WHY THIS WORKS: Hydration has immediate, noticeable benefits. Within days, you'll notice better energy levels, improved focus, and clearer thinking. The signal (sitting at your desk) happens multiple times daily, giving you multiple opportunities to prove your identity.

COMMON OBSTACLES: Forgetting → Keep a full glass on your desk at all times. I don't like plain water → Add lemon, cucumber, or fruit. Frequent bathroom trips → Your body adjusts within a week.

MUST HABIT #3: SLEEP CONSISTENCY

THE COMPLETE LOOP:

I AM Statement: "I am someone who prioritizes rest because it fuels everything I do."

Signal: 9:00 PM alarm on my phone

Identity Reminder: "Sleep is not laziness. It's essential recovery."

Tiny Action: Put phone in another room and change into pajamas

Evidence + Celebration: Track your bedtime in a journal

WHY THIS WORKS: Eliminates two biggest sleep obstacles: phone distraction and lack of bedtime ritual. Once you're in pajamas with no phone, you naturally move toward sleep. Consistent sleep timing affects mood, decision-making, metabolism, and immune function.

MUST HABIT #4: PROTEIN-RICH BREAKFAST

THE COMPLETE LOOP:

> **I AM Statement:** "I am someone who fuels my body with intention."
>
> **Signal:** Right after I finish my morning movement
>
> **Identity Reminder:** "My first meal sets the tone for the entire day"
>
> **Tiny Action:** Eat one protein-rich food (eggs, Greek yogurt, protein shake, or leftovers)
>
> **Evidence + Celebration:** Notice your energy levels throughout the morning

WHY THIS WORKS: Protein stabilizes blood sugar, reduces cravings, provides sustained energy. Carbs/sugar create spike and crash. The benefit is noticeable (stable energy), creating positive reinforcement.

MUST HABIT #5: EVENING STRETCHING

THE COMPLETE LOOP:

> **I AM Statement:** "I am someone who maintains my body for the long term."
>
> **Signal:** Right before I get in bed
>
> **Tiny Action:** Do 3 basic stretches for 30 seconds each (hamstrings, shoulders, neck)
>
> **Evidence + Celebration:** Notice reduced stiffness and tension over time

WHY THIS WORKS: Serves triple duty: maintains flexibility, signals wind-down time, creates mindfulness moment. 90 seconds total—impossible to skip. Feels good (releases tension), so you look forward to it.

Choosing Your First Health Habit

If Health & Vitality is your weakest spoke in the Must Circle of Life, choose ONE of these five habits to start.

How to choose:

- If you struggle with energy and focus: Start with hydration or sleep consistency
- If you struggle with weight or cravings: Start with protein-rich breakfast
- If you struggle with fitness or stamina: Start with daily movement
- If you struggle with tension or stiffness: Start with evening stretching

Whatever you choose, commit to 90 days. Build it to automaticity. Then—and only then—add a second health habit.

RELATIONSHIPS & LOVE: Building Connection and Presence

Relationships are a fundamental pillar of personal growth. They are where meaning lives.

Relationships don't thrive on grand gestures. They thrive on consistent, small acts of care and presence. A relationship that gets 10 minutes of genuine attention every day is stronger than one that gets an expensive vacation once a year.

MUST HABIT #1: DAILY QUALITY CONVERSATION

I AM Statement: "I am a present, connected partner who prioritizes deep conversation."

Signal: Right after dinner | **Identity:** "Connection requires presence" | **Tiny Action:** Put phone in another room, ask one meaningful question | **Evidence:** Notice deeper connection over time

WHY THIS WORKS: Physical removal of phone eliminates biggest distraction. One question ("What was the best part of your day?") creates space for real dialogue. Quality > quantity.

MUST HABIT #2: WEEKLY DATE NIGHT

I AM Statement: "I am someone who invests in my most important relationships."

Signal: Every Friday at 6:00 PM | **Tiny Action:** Put date night on calendar, send calendar invite to partner | **Evidence:** Completed dates tracked in journal

MUST HABIT #3: DAILY GRATITUDE EXPRESSION

I AM Statement: "I am someone who actively appreciates the people I love."

Signal: Before bed | **Tiny Action:** Tell partner one specific thing you appreciate about them | **Evidence:** Notice strengthened connection

WHY THIS WORKS: Research by John Gottman shows that relationships need 5:1 ratio of positive to negative interactions. Daily gratitude creates consistent deposits in the relationship bank.

CAREER & PROFESSIONAL DEVELOPMENT: Building Excellence

Your career reflects pursuit of personal and professional fulfillment. It's about contribution, competence, and continuous growth.

MUST HABIT #1: DAILY DEEP WORK BLOCK

I AM Statement: "I am a professional who produces high-value work through focused attention."

Signal: As soon as I arrive at my desk in the morning | **Identity:** "My most important work deserves my best hours" | **Tiny Action:** Close email, silence phone, work on most important task for 25 minutes

WHY THIS WORKS: Protects peak cognitive hours. Email/messages are reactive. Deep work is proactive. 25 minutes (one Pomodoro) is sustainable. Most important task = highest leverage.

MUST HABIT #2: DAILY SKILL DEVELOPMENT

I AM Statement: "I am someone who grows 1% better every day."

Signal: During lunch break | **Tiny Action:** Watch one 10-minute educational video OR read one article in your field | **Evidence:** Track topics learned in journal

WHY THIS WORKS: 10 minutes daily = 60 hours of learning per year. Lunch break = time already allocated. Tiny investment, compound returns. Career advantage builds invisibly.

MUST HABIT #3: MORNING PRIORITY PLANNING

I AM Statement: "I am someone who works with intention, not reaction."

Signal: Before opening email | **Tiny Action:** Write down top 3 priorities for the day | **Evidence:** Check off completed priorities at end of day

WHY THIS WORKS: Prevents email from hijacking your day. 3 priorities = focused, not overwhelming. Writing crystallizes intention. End-of-day review creates accountability.

90-DAY SNAPSHOT: Health & Vitality Example

Elena had been "starting over on Monday" with her health for fifteen years. She took the Must Circle of Life Assessment and saw what she already knew but had never quantified: Health & Vitality was her weakest spoke by far.

Step 1: Assessment → Domain Choice

On her wheel, Health scored a 3 out of 10 while Career and Relationships sat at 7s and 8s. That made the choice clear. For the next 90 days, Health would be her Must domain.

Step 2: I AM Statement

Using the process from Chapter 2, she chose three values for Health: Energy, Consistency, Self-Respect. She wrote:

"I am someone who honors my body with consistent movement, nutritious food, and real rest because I value energy, consistency, and self-respect."

Step 3: Must Habit Loop

Elena resisted the urge to overhaul everything. In Chapter 5, she built one Must Habit Loop:

- Signal: "After I finish my morning coffee…"
- Identity Reminder: "I am someone who honors my body."
- Tiny Action: "I will walk for 5 minutes outside or in place."
- Evidence/Celebration: Checkmark on the 90-Day Tracker + one deep breath of gratitude.

Days 1–30: Honeymoon

The first month felt easy. The habit was tiny, the weather was good, and the checkmarks on her tracker were satisfying. She occasionally added extra minutes, but her rule stayed the same: 5 minutes counts.

Days 31–66: The Grind

On day 37 it rained. On day 41 she slept badly. On day 49 work exploded. This was the phase Chapter 6 had warned her about. She almost quit, but the Grind now had a name and a purpose. On the hardest days she did "emergency mini-habits"—walking in place in her living room for 60 seconds—because doing something was easier than breaking her identity.

She used the Two-Day Rule from Chapter 9: never miss two days in a row. When she missed a day on day 52, she circled it on her tracker and made the next day nonnegotiable.

Days 67–90: Integration

Somewhere around day 70, she noticed she was putting on her walking shoes without thinking. The signal (finishing coffee) now automatically triggered movement. She extended some walks to 15–20 minutes, but the Must Habit remained "5 minutes counts."

On day 90, Elena re-did the Must Circle of Life Assessment. Health had moved from a 3 to a 6. Nothing else in her life had changed dramatically—same job, same family, same schedule—but her identity had shifted. She no longer saw herself as "someone who can't stick to exercise." She was someone who honors her body. The behavior now fit the identity.

What's Coming in Chapter 8

You now have ready-to-use habit templates for Health & Vitality, Relationships & Love, and Career & Professional Development.

Chapter 8 completes the template collection with the remaining four domains:

- Financial Well-Being
- Personal Growth & Learning
- Spiritual and Peace of Mind
- Community & Legacy

Remember: build one habit at a time. Master it. Then move to the next spoke.

CHAPTER 8

Finance, Growth, Spirit & Legacy Habits

We are what we repeatedly do.
Excellence, then, is not an act, but a habit.
— Will Durant

Sarah had health dialed in. Movement was automatic. Sleep was consistent. Nutrition was solid.

But her Circle of Life was still wobbly. Financial stress kept her up at night. She hadn't read a book in two years. Her spiritual practice had vanished. Community involvement? Zero.

Health was a 9/10. Everything else averaged 3/10.

The wheel was still broken.

Sarah realized that thriving in one domain while neglecting others wasn't balance—it was just a different kind of imbalance.

So she applied the same systematic approach to her weakest spoke: finances.

She chose one habit: daily expense tracking. Built it to automaticity over 90 days. Then moved to personal growth. Then spiritual practice. Then legacy work.

Eighteen months later, every spoke was 7/10 or higher. The wheel rolled smoothly. Life felt complete.

Completing the Circle

This chapter provides habit templates for the final four domains of the Must Circle of Life.

These domains are often neglected because they don't scream for attention like health or career. But they're equally critical to a thriving life:

- Financial Well-Being provides security and freedom
- Personal Growth keeps you expanding
- Spiritual Practice grounds everything else
- Community & Legacy creates meaning beyond yourself

Use the same approach: choose ONE habit from your weakest spoke, build it for 90 days, then move to the next.

FINANCIAL WELL-BEING: Building Security and Freedom

Financial stability provides security and freedom, enabling choices that align with personal goals while reducing stress.

Money doesn't buy happiness—but financial stress destroys it. These habits build the foundation for long-term security.

MUST HABIT #1: DAILY EXPENSE TRACKING

I AM Statement: "I am financially disciplined and aware of every dollar."

Signal: Right before bed | **Tiny Action:** Log today's expenses in app (90 seconds) | **Evidence:** Watch spending awareness increase

WHY THIS WORKS: Awareness precedes change. When you track every expense, you become conscious of spending patterns. "Latte factor" becomes visible. Most people overspend because they're unaware.

MUST HABIT #2: AUTOMATED SAVINGS

I AM Statement: "I am someone who pays myself first."

Signal: Every payday | **Tiny Action:** Set up automatic transfer of $50 to savings account | **Evidence:** Watch savings balance grow

WHY THIS WORKS: Automation removes decision fatigue. "Pay yourself first" principle. Start small ($50), increase as habit solidifies. Invisible wealth-building.

MUST HABIT #3: WEEKLY BUDGET REVIEW

I AM Statement: "I am someone who manages money with intention."

Signal: Every Sunday morning | **Tiny Action:** Review last week's spending, plan this week's budget (15 minutes) | **Evidence:** Notice improved financial control

PERSONAL GROWTH & LEARNING: Continuous Expansion

Personal growth and continuous learning are cornerstones of holistic development. Growth is not optional—stagnation is decline.

MUST HABIT #1: DAILY READING

I AM Statement: "I am a lifelong learner who dedicates time daily to expanding my mind."

Signal: Right before bed | **Tiny Action:** Read one page of a book | **Evidence:** Track books completed

WHY THIS WORKS: One page is impossible to refuse. Momentum usually leads to more. Even if truly just one page, you proved identity. 365 pages/year minimum = multiple books.

MUST HABIT #2: LEARNING JOURNALING

I AM Statement: "I am someone who reflects on and integrates what I learn."

Signal: After reading | **Tiny Action:** Write one insight from what you just learned | **Evidence:** Review insights monthly

WHY THIS WORKS: Writing crystallizes learning. One insight = deep processing. Monthly review = spaced repetition. Knowledge becomes integrated, not forgotten.

MUST HABIT #3: DAILY SKILL PRACTICE

I AM Statement: "I am someone who masters skills through consistent practice."

Signal: During morning coffee | **Tiny Action:** Practice chosen skill for 10 minutes (language, instrument, coding, etc.) | **Evidence:** Track days practiced

WHY THIS WORKS: 10 minutes daily = 60+ hours/year. Compound expertise. Morning = peak cognitive state. Deliberate practice beats sporadic binge sessions.

SPIRITUAL AND PEACE OF MIND: Grounding Everything Else

Inner peace fosters harmony with the self and the transcendent. Without inner peace, external success feels empty.

This domain isn't about religion—it's about the practices that ground you, center you, and connect you to something larger than yourself.

MUST HABIT #1: MORNING MEDITATION

I AM Statement: "I am someone who cultivates inner peace through daily stillness."

Signal: Right after pouring morning coffee | **Tiny Action:** Sit on meditation cushion for 60 seconds | **Evidence:** Mark calendar, notice increased calm

WHY THIS WORKS: 60 seconds removes all excuses. Usually extends naturally to 5-10 minutes. Morning = least resistance. Momentum builds. Even 60 seconds resets nervous system.

Amara - The Data Analyst's Discovery

Amara prided herself on being logical, rational, and evidence-based. She ran statistical models for a living, trusted data over intuition, and scoffed at anything she couldn't quantify. When colleagues talked about meditation or mindfulness, she'd roll her eyes. "I don't need to sit on a cushion staring at a wall," she'd say. "I need to solve real problems."

Then burnout hit at 34. Chronic anxiety. Insomnia. Her doctor suggested meditation. Amara almost laughed—until he showed her the fMRI studies. Brain scans showing reduced amygdala activity, increased prefrontal cortex thickness, and measurable changes in cortisol levels. Data she couldn't dismiss.

She committed to the scientific experiment: 60 seconds of meditation right after pouring her morning coffee. That's it. One minute. She could test anything for one minute. Day one felt ridiculous. Day seven felt slightly less ridiculous. Day thirty, something shifted. She noticed she was calmer in traffic, less reactive in meetings.

By day ninety, Amara was meditating 10 minutes daily without effort. Her anxiety had decreased measurably—she tracked it on a 1-10 scale. Her sleep quality improved from 4/10 to 8/10. But the real transformation was internal: she'd discovered a dimension of herself she didn't know existed. The data analyst had found something her spreadsheets couldn't capture: inner peace.

MUST HABIT #2: GRATITUDE JOURNALING

I AM Statement: "I am someone who actively practices gratitude."

Signal: Right before bed | **Tiny Action:** Write 3 things you're grateful for | **Evidence:** Notice improved mood, perspective

WHY THIS WORKS: Neuroscience shows gratitude rewires brain for positivity. 3 items = specific, not generic. Evening timing improves sleep quality. Shifts focus from lack to abundance.

Michelle - Finding Peace Separate from Religion

Michelle grew up in a rigid religious household. By twenty-five, she'd rejected all of it—the rules, the guilt, the judgment. She threw out spirituality entirely. For sixteen years, she operated purely on ambition and achievement. Marketing director by forty. Six figures. Corner office. Empty.

Her therapist asked: "What brings you peace?" Michelle had no answer. She'd confused rejecting organized religion with rejecting all spiritual practice. But she was exhausted, disconnected, searching for something she couldn't name.

She discovered gratitude journaling through a podcast—three things before bed, written by hand. No prayer required. No deity invoked. Just noticing what was good. She felt skeptical but desperate, so she committed to ninety days.

Week one felt forced. Week four, she started noticing more moments worth recording. By week twelve, gratitude had become automatic—she'd catch herself mentally noting moments of appreciation throughout the day.

Eighteen months later, Michelle practices three spiritual habits: gratitude journaling, nature walks, and breathwork. She's discovered that spiritual doesn't mean religious. It means connected—to herself, to others, to something larger than quarterly earnings. Her therapist noted the transformation: "You found peace without dogma. That's rare.

Maria - From Obligation to Devotion

Maria grew up Catholic. Mass every Sunday. Prayers before bed. But by twenty-nine, it felt mechanical—checkbox spirituality driven by guilt, not genuine connection. She'd pray because she "should," not because she wanted to. Her faith felt like a chore list inherited from her grandmother.

The shift came during a particularly brutal week at the pediatric ICU. A seven-year-old patient asked her: "Do you really believe in God, or do you just say you do?" Maria had no honest answer. She realized she'd been performing religion without experiencing it.

She reframed her identity: Not "I have to pray" but "I am someone who seeks connection with God daily." She started with five minutes of morning prayer—not rote memorization, but actual conversation. Gratitude for breath. Questions about her purpose. Listening in silence.

Six months in, prayer became the most genuine part of her day. She stopped attending church out of obligation and started going because she wanted community. Her rosary wasn't penance—it was meditation with intention.

Maria learned: Religious practice isn't about checking boxes. It's about genuine relationship. The difference between "I should pray" and "I am someone who prays" transformed obligation into devotion.

MUST HABIT #3: WEEKLY NATURE TIME

> **I AM Statement:** "I am someone who reconnects with nature regularly."
>
> **Signal:** Every Saturday morning | **Tiny Action:** Spend 15 minutes outside in nature (walk, sit, observe) | **Evidence:** Track weekly nature visits

WHY THIS WORKS: Nature reduces cortisol, improves mood, provides perspective. Weekly = sustainable, not overwhelming. 15 minutes = accessible. Creates space for reflection.

Yuki - The Burned-Out Executive

Yuki hadn't taken a full vacation in seven years. As VP of Engineering at a tech unicorn, he lived on his phone—emails at 6 AM, Slack until midnight, meetings in between. His wife said he was "always there but never present." His daughter stopped inviting him to school events. At fifty-two, he was having chest pains.

His cardiologist was direct: "Your heart is fine. But your nervous system is in permanent fight-or-flight. You need to ground yourself. Go outside. Touch grass. I'm serious."

Yuki started with fifteen minutes every Saturday morning. Just sitting on a park bench. No phone. No agenda. First few weeks felt agonizing—his brain screamed about wasted time. Then something shifted. Week five, he noticed bird sounds. Week eight, he felt his breathing slow. Week twelve, Saturday morning became the part of the week he most looked forward to.

Two years later, Yuki practices what he calls "radical unplugging": every Saturday, two hours in nature, phone off. His resting heart rate dropped from 82 to 64. He sleeps through the night. But the real change is deeper—he's learned that effectiveness requires rest, that connection requires presence, that success without peace is just expensive suffering.

COMMUNITY & LEGACY: Creating Impact Beyond Yourself

Building connections and leaving meaningful impact ensures continuity, reflecting the cyclical wisdom of collective existence.

Legacy isn't what you leave behind after you die. It's what you build while you're alive.

MUST HABIT #1: MONTHLY VOLUNTEERING

I AM Statement: "I am someone who serves my community consistently."

Signal: First Saturday of each month | **Tiny Action:** Schedule 2 hours of volunteer work, add to calendar | **Evidence:** Track volunteer hours

WHY THIS WORKS: Monthly = sustainable (not overwhelming). Scheduling in advance removes decision fatigue. 2 hours = meaningful contribution. Service creates purpose beyond self.

MUST HABIT #2: WEEKLY MENTORSHIP

I AM Statement: "I am someone who invests in others' growth."

Signal: Every Friday at 4:00 PM | **Tiny Action:** Send one piece of advice or encouragement to someone you mentor | **Evidence:** Notice their growth over time

WHY THIS WORKS: Doesn't require formal mentorship relationship. One message = low barrier. Friday timing = natural reflection point. Compound impact of consistent support.

Harold - The Retired Accountant

Harold retired at sixty-five after forty-two years as a CPA. He'd saved diligently, planned carefully, looked forward to freedom. Six months in, he was depressed. Golf got boring. Gardening filled afternoons but not purpose. His wife gently noted he seemed lost.

The turning point came at a community center breakfast. A college student named Marcus approached him: "You're an accountant, right? Could you help me understand my student loans?" Harold spent ninety minutes explaining amortization, interest capitalization, repayment strategies. Marcus took notes like his life depended on it. At the end, he said: "Nobody's ever explained this to me. Thank you."

Harold felt more alive than he had in months. He created a new identity: "I am someone who passes on knowledge." Every Friday at 4 PM, he'd send advice to someone earlier in their career—via email, coffee meeting, or phone call. Just one person, one hour.

Three years later, Harold has mentored twelve people. Marcus passed his CPA exam and now earns $62,000. Angela started her business with Harold's financial guidance—first year revenue: $180,000. Chen avoided $40,000 in tax mistakes Harold caught.

But Harold's transformation is internal: retirement isn't about stopping. It's about redirecting. His identity shifted from "was an accountant" to "builds accountants." Purpose returned. Depression lifted. Legacy isn't what you leave behind—it's what you build in others while you're still here.

MUST HABIT #3: MONTHLY LEGACY CONTRIBUTION

> **I AM Statement:** "I am someone who contributes to causes larger than myself."
>
> **Signal:** On payday | **Tiny Action:** Donate $25 to a cause you care about | **Evidence:** Track total contributions annually

WHY THIS WORKS: Payday timing = when you have resources. $25 = accessible. Regular giving = identity formation ("I am a contributor"). Compounds into significant annual impact.

Benjamin - The Teacher's Evolution

Benjamin taught high school history for fourteen years. He was good at his job—decent test scores, positive evaluations, and students liked him. But he felt like a cog in a machine. "I'm just preparing them for standardized tests," he told his wife. "Nothing I do matters long-term."

Then he learned about a scholarship fund for first-generation college students in his district. The need was overwhelming: 847 qualified students, only 23 scholarships available. Benjamin felt paralyzed by the scale—until he reframed it. He created a new identity: "I am someone who invests in futures."

Every payday, $25 went to the scholarship fund. Automated. Non-negotiable. He didn't think about it—the money left before he could miss it. It felt insignificant. Then the fund sent an impact report: his $300 annual contribution, combined with others, had funded six full scholarships over four years.

Four years later, Benjamin has contributed $1,200. Combined with 200+ other donors, the fund has awarded forty-two scholarships worth $627,000. One recipient, Maria, became a teacher and returned to the same school where Benjamin teaches.

Benjamin realized: individual impact feels small. Collective impact changes lives. Legacy isn't about being a hero—it's about being one of many who show up consistently.

Building Your Complete System

You now have 19 proven Must Habit templates across all seven domains of the Must Circle of Life.

Here's how to use them:

1. Complete your Circle of Life Assessment (Chapter 3)
2. Identify your weakest spoke
3. Choose ONE habit template from that domain
4. Commit to 90 days using the complete Must Habit Loop
5. Once automatic, move to your next weakest spoke
6. Repeat until all seven spokes are strong

THE COMPOUNDING EFFECT:

If you build one habit every 90 days, within 18-24 months you'll have 7 automatic habits—one in each domain. Your entire Circle of Life will be strong.

That's not wishful thinking. That's systematic transformation.

90-DAY^ SNAPSHOT: Finances & Legacy Example

James had spent years joking that he was "terrible with money." After reading Chapters 1 and 2, the joke stopped being funny. It sounded like an identity he no longer wanted to vote for.

Step 1: Assessment → Domain Choice

His Must Circle of Life Assessment showed decent scores in Career and Relationships, but Financial Well-Being lagged at a 4. He chose

Finances as his 90-day focus, knowing that improving it would also serve his long-term legacy.

Step 2: I AM Statement

In the Financial domain, his values were Stewardship, Clarity, Freedom. He wrote:

"I am financially disciplined. I track my spending, plan ahead, and make decisions that move me toward long-term freedom."

Step 3: Must Habit Loop

From Chapter 5, he built his Must Habit Loop:

- Signal: "After I close my laptop at the end of the workday…"
- Identity Reminder: "I am financially disciplined."
- Tiny Action: "I will open my banking app and track today's transactions in my simple spreadsheet."
- Evidence/Celebration: One line updated in the sheet + a small "Yes, that's who I am" said out loud.

Days 1–30: Honeymoon

The first month was surprisingly pleasant. Seeing his spending in one place gave him a sense of control he hadn't felt in years. He occasionally added 5 minutes to plan tomorrow's spending, but the nonnegotiable was still "track today."

Days 31–66: The Grind

Around week six, the novelty wore off. On travel days and late nights, the last thing he wanted to do was look at money. Twice he forgot. The old "I'm terrible with money" script tried to return.

Chapter 9's Two-Day Rule saved the habit. Any time he missed, he made the very next day ultra-simple: open the app, enter just one transaction, mark the box on his tracker. Even in the Grind, the tiny action was still doable.

Days 67–90: Integration

By week ten, the loop felt automatic. Laptop closed → banking app opened. He no longer argued with himself about whether to track; he simply did what financially disciplined people do.

On day 90, he reviewed three months of data. Without setting a "pay off X dollars" goal, he had:

- Stopped several small subscriptions he never used.
- Redirected that money into an automatic weekly transfer to savings.
- Paid down more on his credit card than in any previous quarter.

More importantly, he no longer introduced himself—even as a joke—as "bad with money." He had 90 days of proof that he was someone who tracks every dollar and makes thoughtful choices. The habit had become part of his identity, and the financial results were following.

What's Coming in Part IV

You now have the complete template library. But what happens when you break a streak? How do you design your environment for success? What advanced strategies accelerate habit formation?

Part IV covers Advanced Strategies:

- Chapter 9: When You Break the Streak (recovery strategies)
- Chapter 10: Environment Design & Advanced Tactics
- Chapter 11: The Complete System (putting it all together)

Templates remove decision fatigue.

Execution builds automaticity.

Consistency creates transformation.

PART IV
ADVANCED STRATEGIES

CHAPTER 9

When You Break the Streak

*Our greatest glory is not in never falling,
but in rising every time we fall.*
— Confucius

Derek had a 47-day meditation streak.

Every single morning for 47 days, he sat on his cushion. The habit felt automatic. He was in Phase 2, approaching the integration phase. Victory was close.

Then he got sick.

Day 48: Flu hit hard. Fever, body aches, complete exhaustion. No meditation. Day 49: Still sick. No meditation. Day 50: Feeling better, but the momentum was gone.

Derek faced a choice.

Option 1: Restart from day 1. This felt devastating. All that progress, erased. The thought made him not want to start again.

Option 2: Give up entirely. "I lost the streak anyway. What's the point?"

Option 3: Use the Two-Day Rule.

On day 51, Derek meditated. He didn't restart his count. He marked it as day 48. Because the rule is simple: you can miss one day. You cannot miss two days in a row.

The Two-Day Rule saved his habit. Instead of catastrophizing the break, he treated it as a minor interruption. The streak didn't die. It paused.

Ninety days after he started (not 90 consecutive days—90 total attempts), meditation was automatic. The two sick days didn't break the habit. They tested it. And it survived.

Why Streaks Die (And How to Save Them)

You will break your streak.

Not might. Will.

Life happens. You get sick. You travel. You have a crisis. You forget. You're human.

The question isn't whether you'll break the streak. The question is: what do you do when you break it?

Most people catastrophize. They see one missed day as total failure. They abandon the habit entirely. They prove the all-or-nothing mentality that sabotages long-term success.

But research shows that missing one day—or even two—doesn't significantly impact habit formation. What kills habits is the psychological spiral that follows the break.

The Two-Day Rule: Your Streak Insurance

The Two-Day Rule is simple but powerful:

You can miss one day.

You cannot miss two days in a row.

MUST HABITS

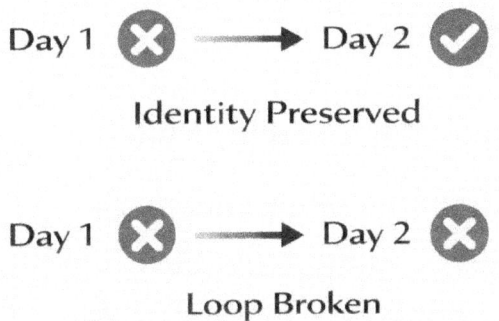

Identity Preserved

Loop Broken

That's it. One miss is human. Two consecutive misses is a pattern. And patterns become habits—including the habit of not doing your habit.

WHY THIS WORKS:

The Two-Day Rule eliminates catastrophic thinking. One missed day isn't failure—it's life. But it creates urgency for the next day. You know you must show up tomorrow, or the pattern breaks.

It also protects the neural pathway. Research shows that habits can survive occasional interruptions without significant degradation. The neural encoding remains intact for 24-48 hours. But after two consecutive misses, the pathway begins weakening.

THE NEUROSCIENCE: What Happens When You Miss Days

When you perform a habit, you strengthen the neural pathway through long-term potentiation (LTP). Miss one day, and the pathway remains intact. Miss two consecutive days, and synaptic connections begin weakening through long-term depression (LTD)—the opposite process.

This is why the Two-Day Rule is neurologically sound: it protects the pathway during brief interruptions while preventing degradation from extended breaks. One rest day maintains strength, but three consecutive rest days begin detraining.

How to Apply the Two-Day Rule

STEP 1: Accept That You'll Miss Days

Plan for imperfection. Your goal isn't perfection—it's consistency over time. A 90-day habit with 5 missed days (94% completion) is far more successful than a 30-day perfect streak followed by abandonment.

STEP 2: Track Your Misses

Mark missed days clearly on your tracker. Visual accountability shows at a glance if you're approaching two consecutive misses.

STEP 3: Create Emergency Mini-Habits

For sick days, travel, or crisis, have an even smaller version ready:

- Full: 30-min workout → Emergency: 5 pushups
- Full: 20-min meditation → Emergency: 3 deep breaths
- Full: Write 500 words → Emergency: Write one sentence
- Full: Read 20 pages → Emergency: Read one paragraph

The emergency version still counts. It proves identity. It maintains the pathway. It keeps the streak alive.

STEP 4: Never Miss Twice

If you missed yesterday, today is non-negotiable. No excuses. Execute the emergency mini-habit minimum.

This is the rule that protects everything. One miss is forgivable. Two consecutive misses starts the death spiral.

Common Streak-Breaking Scenarios (And How to Recover)

SCENARIO 1: You Get Sick

What happens: Fever, exhaustion, or injury makes your normal habit impossible.

The mistake: Skipping entirely and losing momentum.

The solution: Execute the emergency mini-habit. If you physically can't, give yourself one day. On day two, do the absolute minimum—even if it's just thinking about your I AM Statement for 10 seconds.

SCENARIO 2: You're Traveling

What happens: Routine disrupted. Signal doesn't happen. Environment unfamiliar.

The mistake: Waiting until you're home to restart.

The solution: Adapt the habit to your travel context. Can't go to gym? Do 10 pushups in hotel room. Can't meditate in normal space? Meditate anywhere. Adaptation > abandonment.

SCENARIO 3: Life Crisis Hits

What happens: Death, job loss, relationship end, major emergency.

The mistake: Abandoning all habits because "bigger things matter right now."

The solution: Your habits are your anchor during crisis. Scale down, don't eliminate. The structure helps. The identity proof helps. Even 60 seconds provides stability when everything else is chaos.

SCENARIO 4: You Simply Forgot

What happens: Life got busy. The signal didn't happen. You forgot.

The mistake: Beating yourself up, catastrophizing, quitting.

The solution: Forgive immediately. Execute the habit right now if possible. If not, execute tomorrow without fail. One forgotten day is data—it means your signal needs strengthening.

The Comeback Formula: Getting Back on Track

When you break a streak, use this 4-step comeback formula:

STEP 1: Acknowledge Without Judgment

Say out loud: "I missed my habit. That's data, not disaster."

Notice the emotion (frustration, guilt, disappointment) without drowning in it. You're human. Humans miss things. This doesn't define you.

STEP 2: Diagnose the Cause

Ask: Why did I miss?

- Signal didn't happen? Strengthen the signal.
- Forgot entirely? Add a backup reminder.
- Too tired/busy? Simplify the tiny action.
- Sick/traveling? Use emergency mini-habit next time.

Every miss is data. Use it to improve the system.

STEP 3: Execute Immediately (If Possible)

If you realize you missed at 11 PM, do the emergency mini-habit before bed. Better late than never.

If it's truly impossible today, commit to tomorrow. But make it non-negotiable.

STEP 4: Recommit to Your Identity

Say your I AM Statement out loud. Remind yourself who you are.

"I am someone who moves my body daily." One missed day doesn't change that. Tomorrow, you prove it again.

EXAMPLE: The Power of the Comeback

> *Nina had a 52-day writing streak. Then she missed a day. Then another. By day three, she felt defeated. "I'll just start over next month."*
>
> *But she remembered the Two-Day Rule. She'd already missed two days. Day four was do-or-die.*
>
> *On day four, she wrote one sentence. Then one more. Then a paragraph. The comeback felt harder than starting. But she did it.*
>
> *That comeback was more valuable than the 52-day streak. It taught her that habits don't die from one break. They die from giving up after the break.*

What's Coming in Chapter 10

You now know how to save your streaks when life disrupts them. But what if you could prevent most disruptions entirely?

Chapter 10 reveals advanced strategies that make habits even easier:

- Environment design (make good habits invisible to resist)
- Temptation bundling (pair habits with pleasures)
- Implementation intentions (if-then planning)
- Social accountability (leverage community)
- Keystone habits (habits that trigger other habits)
- Habit scaling (progressive complexity)

STEPHEN RUE

Missing once is human.

Missing twice is a pattern.

The comeback is everything.

CHAPTER 10

Environment Design & Advanced Tactics

Environment is the invisible hand that shapes human behavior.

— James Clear

Rachel wanted to read more. She set a goal: 30 minutes nightly.

Week 1: Read 3 out of 7 nights. Week 2: Read 2 out of 7 nights. Week 3: Read once.

The problem wasn't willpower. It was environment.

Every evening, she'd sit on the couch to read. Her phone was next to her. The TV remote was on the coffee table. Netflix auto-played.

She was trying to build a reading habit in an environment designed for distraction.

Then she redesigned everything:

- Moved the book to her bedside table (visible cue)
- Put her phone in another room before 9 PM (removed obstacle)
- Created a reading chair in the corner (dedicated space)
- Kept TV remote in a drawer (friction for distraction)

Week 4: Read 6 out of 7 nights. Week 5: Read 7 out of 7 nights.

Same person. Same goal. Different environment. Different results.

Why Environment Matters More Than Willpower

You are not battling your lack of discipline. You are battling your environment.

Every environment has default behaviors. Sit on the couch near the TV? The default is watching Netflix. Sit at a desk with your phone visible? The default is scrolling.

Willpower is trying to resist the defaults. Environment design is changing the defaults.

The most successful habit-builders don't rely on self-control. They design environments where the right choice is the easy choice.

STRATEGY #1: Environment Design

The Two Rules of Environment Design:

Rule 1: Make good habits obvious.

If you want to exercise, put your workout clothes where you'll see them immediately when you wake up.

If you want to read, place the book on your pillow.

If you want to eat healthy, put fruit in a visible bowl on the counter.

Rule 2: Make bad habits invisible.

If you want to stop scrolling social media, delete apps from your phone.

If you want to eat less junk food, don't keep it in the house.

If you want to watch less TV, unplug it and put the remote in a drawer.

PRACTICAL EXAMPLES:

For Daily Movement:

- Put workout clothes on your bedroom floor the night before
- Leave running shoes by the door
- Keep resistance bands next to your desk
- Set up a dedicated workout space (even just a yoga mat)

For Daily Reading:

- Keep book on pillow
- Put phone in another room
- Create a reading chair/corner
- Keep TV remote hidden

STRATEGY #2: Temptation Bundling

Temptation bundling is pairing something you need to do with something you want to do.

Formula: Only do [THING YOU LOVE] while doing [HABIT YOU'RE BUILDING].

EXAMPLES:

- Only watch your favorite show while on the treadmill
- Only listen to audiobooks while commuting

- Only drink your premium coffee while doing morning journaling
- Only get a pedicure while reviewing your budget
- Only eat at your favorite restaurant while having weekly planning session

WHY THIS WORKS: Your brain begins to crave the habit because it's associated with pleasure. The treadmill becomes the gateway to your favorite show. The habit becomes the reward itself.

STRATEGY #3: Implementation Intentions (If-Then Planning)

Implementation intentions are if-then plans that automate decision-making.

Formula: If [SITUATION], then I will [RESPONSE].

Research by Peter Gollwitzer shows that people who use implementation intentions are 2-3x more likely to follow through on goals.

EXAMPLES:

- If I feel like skipping my workout, then I will do just 5 pushups
- If someone offers me junk food, then I will say "No thanks, I'm eating clean this week"
- If I'm tempted to check my phone during dinner, then I will take 3 deep breaths
- If I miss my morning meditation, then I will meditate for 60 seconds before bed
- If I'm too tired to read, then I will read just one paragraph

WHY THIS WORKS: Pre-decision eliminates decision fatigue. When the situation arrives, you don't deliberate. You execute the pre-planned response.

STRATEGY #4: Social Accountability

Humans are social creatures. We care deeply about what others think. Use this to your advantage.

THREE LEVELS OF SOCIAL ACCOUNTABILITY:

Level 1: Public Declaration

Tell people about your habit. Post on social media. Share with friends.

Why it works: Creates social pressure. You don't want to be the person who said they'd do something and didn't.

Level 2: Accountability Partner

Find one person who's building a similar habit. Check in daily. Share your progress.

Why it works: Daily check-ins create immediate accountability. You don't want to disappoint your partner.

Level 3: Habit Contract with Stakes

Write a contract: "If I miss my habit X days this month, I will donate $100 to a cause I hate." Give it to a friend to enforce.

Why it works: Loss aversion is powerful. The pain of losing money is greater than the pleasure of gaining it.

STRATEGY #5: Keystone Habits

Keystone habits are habits that trigger cascades of other positive behaviors.

Build one keystone habit, and multiple other habits often follow automatically.

COMMON KEYSTONE HABITS:

1. Daily Exercise

When people start exercising regularly, they often:

- Eat healthier (don't want to waste the workout)
- Sleep better (physical fatigue improves sleep)
- Manage stress better (exercise reduces cortisol)
- Become more productive (increased energy and focus)

2. Morning Routine

When people establish a morning routine, they often:

- Go to bed earlier (to wake up for the routine)
- Eat breakfast (it's part of the routine)
- Feel more in control all day (strong start = strong finish)

3. Daily Meditation

When people meditate regularly, they often:

- Become more mindful about food choices
- React less emotionally in relationships
- Make better financial decisions
- Increase overall self-discipline

WHY THIS WORKS: Keystone habits create identity shifts. "I'm someone who exercises" becomes "I'm someone who takes care of myself." That broader identity triggers multiple aligned behaviors.

STRATEGY #6: Habit Scaling (Progressive Complexity)

Don't keep your habit tiny forever. Once it's automatic (66-90 days), scale it up.

THE SCALING TIMELINE:

Days 1-30: Master the Tiny Action

Focus on consistency, not intensity. Put on workout clothes. Write one sentence. Read one page.

Days 31-66: Increase Slightly

Once the tiny action feels automatic, add small increments:

- Workout clothes → Walk to end of street
- One sentence → One paragraph
- One page → Five pages

Days 67-90: Reach Target Intensity

Now scale to your full desired habit:

- Walk to street → Full 30-minute workout
- One paragraph → 500 words
- Five pages → 30 minutes of reading

IMPORTANT: Always keep the tiny action as your fallback. On hard days, you can always return to "just put on the clothes" or "just one sentence." That still counts.

EXAMPLE: Scaling in Action

> Marcus started with "put on workout clothes" for 30 days. Day 31, he added "walk to the end of the street." Still tiny. Still easy.
>
> Day 67, he scaled to "walk around the block." Day 90, "full 30-minute workout."
>
> One year later, Marcus was working out 6 days/week. But on sick days? He still just put on the clothes. The tiny action remained his anchor.

Combining Strategies for Maximum Impact

The real power comes from stacking these strategies together.

EXAMPLE: Building an Unstoppable Morning Meditation Habit

- Environment Design: Put meditation cushion next to bed (obvious)
- Temptation Bundling: Only drink premium coffee after meditation
- Implementation Intention: "If I feel like skipping, I'll sit for just 60 seconds"
- Social Accountability: Daily check-in with meditation accountability partner
- Keystone Effect: Meditation improves everything else (mindfulness cascades)
- Habit Scaling: Days 1-30 = 60 seconds, Days 31-66 = 5 minutes, Days 67+ = 20 minutes

With all six strategies working together, the habit becomes nearly inevitable.

TOOL: The Strategy Selector

Use this guide to choose which strategies to apply to your habit:

If your main challenge is:

- "I forget to do it" → Environment Design (make it obvious)
- "It feels boring" → Temptation Bundling (pair with pleasure)
- "I give up when obstacles arise" → Implementation Intentions (pre-plan responses)
- "I lack motivation" → Social Accountability (external pressure)

- "I want faster transformation" → Keystone Habits (cascading effects)
- "I've mastered the tiny action" → Habit Scaling (increase intensity)

What's Coming in Chapter 11

You now have six advanced strategies to accelerate habit formation and prevent disruption.

Chapter 11 brings everything together: the complete Must Habits system, your 90-day transformation plan, and how to build a life that thrives in all seven domains.

Willpower is fighting your environment.

Strategy is designing your environment.

Excellence is the result.

CHAPTER 11

The Complete Must Habits System

*You do not rise to the level of your goals.
You fall to the level of your systems.*
— James Clear

Maria sat with her Circle of Life assessment. Every spoke was below 5/10.

Health: 4/10. Relationships: 3/10. Career: 5/10. Finances: 2/10. Growth: 3/10. Spiritual: 2/10. Legacy: 1/10.

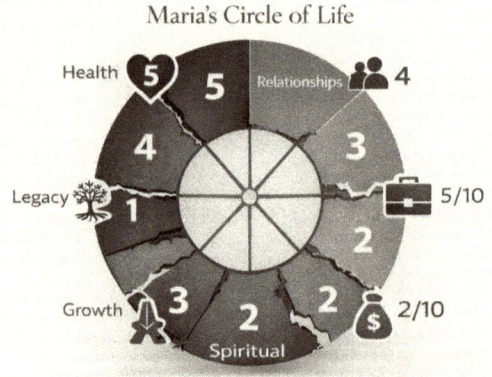

Maria sat with her Circle of Life assessment. Every spoke was below 5/10.
Health: 4/10, Relationships: 3/10, Career: 5/10, Finances: 2/10, Growth: 3/10, 2/10.
Spiritual: 2/10, Legacy: 1/10.

The wheel was broken in seven places.

She could have been overwhelmed. She could have tried to fix everything at once. She could have given up entirely.

Instead, she chose the system.

Month 1-3: Health. Daily movement habit. Put on workout clothes after coffee. By day 90, automatic.

Month 4-6: Finances. Daily expense tracking. Log expenses before bed. By day 180, second habit automatic.

Month 7-9: Spiritual. Morning meditation. Sit for 60 seconds after coffee. By day 270, third habit automatic.

The pattern continued. One habit every 90 days. One spoke at a time.

Twenty-four months later, Maria retook the assessment:

Health: 8/10. Relationships: 7/10. Career: 8/10. Finances: 7/10. Growth: 7/10. Spiritual: 8/10. Legacy: 6/10.

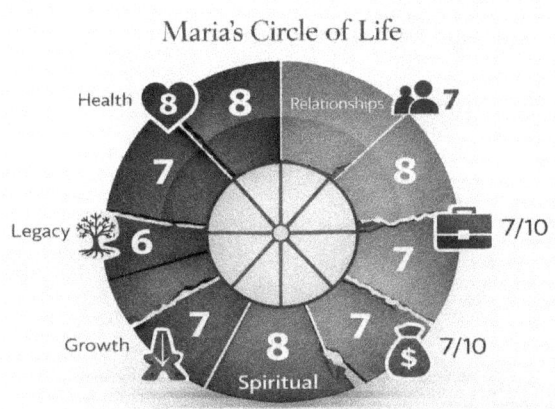

Twenty-four months later, Maria retook the assessment:
Heath: 8/10, Relationships: 7/10, Career: 8/10, Finances: 7/10.
Growth: 7/10, Spiritual: 8/10, Legacy: 6/10.

The wheel rolled smoothly. Not because she had a breakthrough moment. Because she had a system.

The Power of Systems Over Goals

Goals tell you where you want to go. Systems get you there.

Goals are about results. Systems are about processes.

Goals create an "all or nothing" mentality—you either achieve the goal or you don't. Systems create continuous improvement—you get better every day regardless of the outcome.

The Must Habits system is your operating system for continuous transformation.

It doesn't rely on motivation. It doesn't require perfection. It simply requires showing up consistently for your identity, one tiny action at a time.

The Complete Must Habits System: A Visual Overview

Here's how all the pieces fit together:

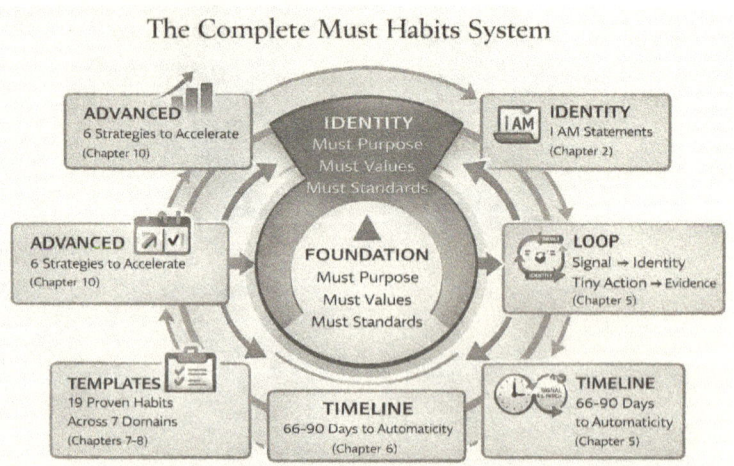

The 10 Steps to Building Your First Must Habit

Use this step-by-step process to build your first habit (and every habit after that):

STEP 1: Complete Your Circle of Life Assessment

Rate yourself 1-10 in each of the seven domains:

- Health & Vitality
- Relationships & Love
- Career & Professional Development
- Financial Well-Being
- Personal Growth & Learning
- Spiritual and Peace of Mind
- Community & Legacy

Be brutally honest. This assessment determines your starting point.

STEP 2: Identify Your Weakest Spoke

Look at your scores. Which domain is lowest?

That's where you start. Not because it's easy, but because strengthening your weakest spoke has the greatest impact on your overall well-being.

STEP 3: Write Your I AM Statement for That Domain

Using the framework from Chapter 2, craft your identity statement.

Formula: "I am someone who [identity] because [values]."

Example: "I am someone who honors my body through consistent movement because I value energy, longevity, and self-respect."

STEP 4: Choose ONE Must Action

From the templates in Chapters 7-8, select ONE habit that would prove your I AM Statement.

Or design your own using the four criteria:

- Aligned with your I AM Statement
- Observable and concrete
- Small enough to do daily (<2 minutes)
- Creates immediate feedback

STEP 5: Design Your Must Habit Loop

Using the framework from Chapter 5, build your complete loop:

> **Signal:** After I _____ (existing behavior or specific time)
>
> **Identity Reminder:** "I am someone who _____"
>
> **Tiny Action:** I will _____ (must be <2 minutes)
>
> **Evidence + Celebration:** I will track by _____ and celebrate by _____

STEP 6: Design Your Environment

From Chapter 10, apply environment design:

- Make the good habit obvious (what will you see?)
- Make bad habits invisible (what will you remove?)
- Reduce friction for the good habit (what makes it easier?)
- Increase friction for bad habits (what makes them harder?)

STEP 7: Create Your Emergency Mini-Habit

From Chapter 9, decide on your emergency version for sick days, travel, or crisis:

My full habit: _____

My emergency mini-habit: _____

STEP 8: Choose Your Advanced Strategies

From Chapter 10, select 1-3 strategies to apply:

- Temptation bundling (if it feels boring)
- Implementation intentions (if obstacles derail you)
- Social accountability (if you lack motivation)

STEP 9: Commit to 90 Days

Mark your calendar:

Start Date: _____

Day 66 (Average Automaticity): _____

Day 90 (Completion): _____

Remember the Two-Day Rule: You can miss one day. You cannot miss two days in a row.

STEP 10: Execute Daily (No Matter What)

Every single day for 90 days:

1. When your signal appears, pause for 3 seconds
2. Say your I AM Statement (out loud or in your mind)
3. Execute your tiny action

4. Mark it on your tracker
5. Celebrate immediately

That's it. That's the system.

Simple? Yes. Easy? Not always. Effective? Absolutely.

The Transformation Roadmaps: 12-Month and 24-Month Plans

Now that you understand the system, here's how to apply it to transform your entire Circle of Life.

THE 12-MONTH ROADMAP (4 Habits)

This roadmap builds four foundational habits in one year—one every 90 days.

Months 1-3: Health & Vitality

Why start here: Health is the foundation. Without energy and vitality, everything else becomes harder.

> *Recommended habit:* Daily Movement (put on workout clothes after coffee)
>
> *Expected outcome:* By day 90, movement is automatic. Energy increases. Mood improves. Sleep quality enhances.

Months 4-6: Financial Well-Being

Why second: Financial stress undermines everything. Building awareness and control creates security.

> *Recommended habit:* Daily Expense Tracking (log expenses before bed)

Expected outcome: By day 180, financial awareness is automatic. Spending patterns clear. Control increases.

Months 7-9: Relationships & Love

Why third: With health and finances stabilizing, invest in connection. Strong relationships multiply joy.

Recommended habit: Daily Quality Conversation (phone away after dinner, ask one meaningful question)

Expected outcome: By day 270, presence is automatic. Relationship depth increases. Connection strengthens.

Months 10-12: Spiritual and Peace of Mind

Why fourth: With physical, financial, and relational foundations in place, cultivate inner peace. This grounds everything.

Recommended habit: Morning Meditation (sit for 60 seconds after coffee)

Expected outcome: By day 360, stillness is automatic. Stress decreases. Clarity increases. Peace deepens.

12-Month Result: Four automatic habits. Four strengthened spokes. Significantly improved wheel.

THE 24-MONTH ROADMAP (7+ Habits)

This roadmap strengthens all seven spokes—one habit every 90 days, plus accelerated growth in year two.

Year One (Months 1-12): Follow the 12-month roadmap above (Health → Finance → Relationships → Spiritual)

Months 13-15: Career & Professional Development

Recommended habit: Daily Deep Work Block (25 minutes on most important task before email)

Months 16-18: Personal Growth & Learning

Recommended habit: Daily Reading (one page before bed)

Months 19-21: Community & Legacy

Recommended habit: Monthly Volunteering (2 hours first Saturday of each month)

Months 22-24: Scale and Deepen

Option 1: Add a second habit to your weakest spoke (e.g., add sleep consistency to Health)

Option 2: Scale existing habits to higher intensity (e.g., 60-second meditation → 20 minutes)

Option 3: Focus on keystone habits that trigger multiple behaviors

24-Month Result: Seven automatic habits minimum. All seven spokes strengthened. Wheel rolling smoothly.

Common Challenges (And How to Overcome Them)

CHALLENGE 1: "I want to change faster. Can I build multiple habits simultaneously?"

The temptation: Build 3-5 habits at once to accelerate transformation.

The reality: Your prefrontal cortex has limited bandwidth. Multiple new habits overload the system. Research shows 90% failure rate when building multiple habits simultaneously vs. 70-80% success with one habit at a time.

The solution: Focus ruthlessly on ONE habit until automatic (66-90 days). Then add the next. Sequential habit-building is slower initially but sustainable long-term.

CHALLENGE 2: "My weakest spoke isn't Health—it's [other domain]. Should I still start there?"

The recommendation: The roadmaps suggest starting with Health because it creates foundation for everything else.

The reality: If Health is already strong (7/10+) but Finances are critical (2/10), start with Finances. Always start with your actual weakest spoke.

The principle: Strengthen what's weakest first. The roadmaps are templates, not mandates. Adapt to your reality.

CHALLENGE 3: "I built the habit, but I'm not seeing results. Should I quit?"

The frustration: You've meditated for 45 days and don't feel more peaceful. You've exercised for 60 days and haven't lost weight.

The reality: Results lag behind actions. James Clear: "Habits are the compound interest of self-improvement." The payoff is delayed but guaranteed.

The solution: Focus on the process, not the outcome. You're not building habits for 90-day results. You're building them for lifetime transformation. Trust the compound effect.

CHALLENGE 4: "Life exploded. My habits collapsed. Do I start over?"

The situation: Major life event (death, job loss, health crisis, move) disrupted everything.

The mistake: Abandoning all habits entirely and "waiting until things calm down."

The solution: Scale down to emergency mini-habits. Even 10 seconds of your habit provides anchor during chaos. Maintain the identity even if you reduce intensity. When life stabilizes, scale back up.

The Final Step: Begin

You now have everything you need:

- The science of habit formation
- The Must Habit Loop framework
- 19 proven habit templates
- Recovery strategies for when you break streaks
- Advanced tactics to accelerate progress
- A complete 12-month and 24-month transformation roadmap

Knowledge without action is useless.

Close this book. Complete your Circle of Life assessment. Choose your weakest spoke. Design your first Must Habit Loop.

Then execute.

Tomorrow morning, when your signal appears, you will have a choice:

Continue being who you've been, or prove who you're becoming.

The tiny action you take tomorrow doesn't matter because it's big. It matters because it's proof.

Proof that you are who you say you are.

Systems beat goals.

Identity beats motivation.

Daily proof beats promises.

You are one habit away from transformation.

CONCLUSION

Your Transformation Begins Today

You opened this book because something needs to change.

Maybe your Circle of Life is broken. Maybe you know who you want to be but don't know how to get there. Maybe you've tried to change before and failed.

You're not alone.

Millions of people set goals every year. Millions try to build better habits. And millions fail—not because they lack discipline, but because they lack a system.

Now you have the system.

What You've Learned

In this book, you discovered:

Why goals fail and habits succeed. Goals focus on outcomes. Habits encode identity. When you change who you are, outcomes become inevitable.

The power of I AM Statements. Your habits must flow from your identity, not your aspirations. "I am someone who..." is more powerful than "I want to..."

The Must Circle of Life framework. True success requires balance across all seven domains. Strengthen your weakest spoke first.

How to enter the Must Zone. The sweet spot between comfort and panic where growth feels aligned, not forced.

The Must Habit Loop. Signal → Identity → Tiny Action → Evidence + Celebration. This is how your brain encodes automaticity.

The truth about timelines. Not 21 days. Not 30 days. An average of 66 days, with a range of 18-254 days depending on complexity. Commit to 90 days.

Ready-to-use templates. Nineteen proven habits across all seven domains. You don't have to invent—just implement.

How to save broken streaks. The Two-Day Rule: you can miss one day, but you cannot miss two days in a row.

Advanced strategies. Environment design, temptation bundling, implementation intentions, social accountability, keystone habits, and habit scaling.

The complete transformation roadmap. Twelve months to four automatic habits. Twenty-four months to a completely balanced Circle of Life.

The Choice Ahead

You now stand at a crossroads.

One path leads back to your old patterns. You close this book, feel inspired for a few days, then return to exactly who you were. The broken wheel keeps wobbling.

The other path requires commitment. Tomorrow morning, when your alarm goes off or your coffee brews, you pause for three seconds. You say your I AM Statement. You execute your tiny action. You mark it on your tracker. You celebrate.

Then you do it again the next day. And the day after that.

Not because you feel motivated. Because it's who you are.

Ninety days from now, that tiny action will be automatic. The behavior that once required willpower will require none. The identity you declared will be proven.

One hundred eighty days from now, you'll have two automatic habits. Two strengthened spokes.

Three hundred sixty days from now, you'll have four.

Seven hundred thirty days from now, your entire Circle of Life will be transformed.

Not through heroic effort. Through systematic execution.

Remember This

When you're in Phase 2 (the grind) and it still feels hard:

This is normal. You're not failing. You're early. Keep showing up.

When you break your streak:

One miss is human. Execute tomorrow. Never miss twice.

When you don't see results yet:

Results lag behind actions. Trust the compound effect. The payoff is delayed but guaranteed.

When life gets chaotic:

Scale to your emergency mini-habit. Even 10 seconds proves identity and maintains the pathway.

When you're tempted to add more habits too soon:

> *Sequential beats simultaneous. Master one habit before adding the next.*

Your Must Purpose Awaits

This book is part of the Must Personal Development Book Series:

- Must: Becoming the Person You Are Meant to Be (discovering your purpose)
- Must Goals: Achieving What Truly Matters (setting aligned goals)
- Must Habits: Building the Life You Want (making it automatic)

Each book serves a different function:

Must answers: **Who am I meant to be?**

Must Goals answers: **What should I achieve?**

Must Habits answers: **How do I become that person?**

Must Year answers: **How do I reflect and improve various areas of my life?**

Must Book Guided Journal answers: **How do I express my positive dynamic changes in my life**

Together, they form a complete system for living your Must life—the life you were meant to live.

But knowledge means nothing without execution.

The First Step

Close this book.

Open your calendar or journal.

MUST HABITS

Complete your Circle of Life assessment. Rate yourself 1-10 in all seven domains.

Identify your weakest spoke.

Choose ONE habit from that domain—or design your own using the four criteria.

Build your Must Habit Loop: Signal → Identity → Tiny Action → Evidence + Celebration.

Mark Day 90 on your calendar.

Then begin.

Tomorrow morning, you will prove who you are.

Not through a grand gesture. Through a tiny action.

That tiny action is a vote for your identity. One vote doesn't determine the election. But ninety votes do.

You are ninety days away from automatic transformation.

You are one year away from four powerful habits.

You are two years away from a completely balanced life.

But it all begins with tomorrow's tiny action.

Your transformation doesn't require more motivation.

It doesn't require more willpower.

It doesn't require perfection.

It requires one thing:

Daily proof of who you are.

Begin.

APPENDICES

APPENDIX A

The Must Habits Toolkit

This appendix contains all the practical tools, worksheets, and trackers referenced throughout the book. Photocopy these pages or download digital versions at www.mustbook.com/tools

TOOL 1: The Circle of Life Assessment

Use this assessment to evaluate your current state across all seven domains.

Instructions: Rate yourself 1-10 in each domain. Be brutally honest. This is your starting point.

LIFE DOMAIN	RATING (1-10)	KEY QUESTION
Health & Vitality		Do I consistently care for my body through movement, nutrition, and rest?
Relationships & Love		Do I invest quality time in my most important relationships?
Career & Professional		Am I growing in my career and contributing meaningfully?

Financial Well-Being		Do I manage money wisely and feel financially secure?
Personal Growth		Am I learning and expanding my knowledge and skills?
Spiritual & Peace		Do I have practices that ground me and cultivate inner peace?
Community & Legacy		Am I contributing to something larger than myself?

Rating Scale:

- 1-3: Critically neglected (urgent attention needed)
- 4-6: Functional but not thriving (needs improvement)
- 7-8: Doing well (maintenance mode)
- 9-10: Flourishing (exceptional)

MY WEAKEST SPOKE: _____

This is where I will start building my first Must Habit.

TOOL 2: The I AM Statement Builder

Use this worksheet to craft a powerful I AM Statement for your chosen domain.

STEP 1: Identify the domain

My chosen domain: _____

STEP 2: Define the identity

Who am I in this domain? (Use present tense, as if already true)

_____

_____

STEP 3: Connect to your values

Why does this identity matter to me?

_____

_____

STEP 4: Write your complete I AM Statement

Formula: "I am someone who [identity] because [values]."

_____

_____

_____

Examples:

- "I am someone who honors my body through consistent movement because I value energy, longevity, and self-respect."

- *"I am someone who manages money with intention because I value security, freedom, and peace of mind."*
- *"I am a present, connected parent who prioritizes quality time because I value deep relationships and creating lasting memories."*

Habit Awareness Snapshot

Optional Tool: Habit Awareness Snapshot

List 5 daily behaviors in your weakest spoke. Which prove your desired identity? Which contradict it?

Daily Behavior	✓ Proves My Desired Identity	✗ Contradicts My Desired Identity
1.	☑	☒
2.	☑	☒
3.	☑	☒
4.	☑	☒
5.	☑	☒
6.	☑	☒

TOOL 3: The Must Habit Loop Designer

Use this template to design your complete habit loop.

STEP 1: THE SIGNAL (What triggers this habit?)

Choose a signal that is already happening in your routine:

After I: _____

When: _____

Right before I: _____

STEP 2: THE IDENTITY REMINDER (What will I think?)

Write your I AM Statement here:

"I am someone who _____

_____"

STEP 3: THE TINY ACTION (What will I do? Must be <2 minutes)

I will: _____

_____

Time required: _____ seconds/minutes (must be under 2 minutes)

STEP 4: EVIDENCE + CELEBRATION (How will I track and celebrate?)

I will track by: _____

I will celebrate by: _____

MUST HABITS

MY 90-DAY COMMITMENT:

Start date: _____

Day 66 (average automaticity): _____

Day 90 (completion): _____

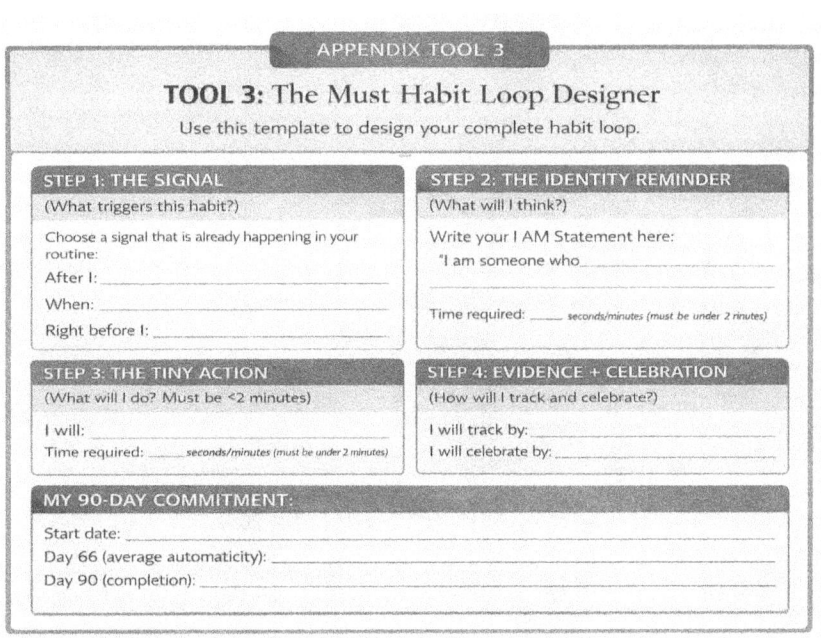

Optional Tool:
Environment That Protects Identity

Does your environment make it harder to take Must Action? Take a moment to review the setup of your surroundings.

What makes my Must Action harder than it needs to be?
- [x] _____
- [x] _____

What can I remove, automate, or pre-stage?
- [x] _____
- [x] _____
- [x] _____

Optional Tool:
Celebration Ideas
(Evidence + Celebration)

Celebration Ideas (Non-food, Non-destructive):
- Verbal self-acknowledgment
- Checkmark ritual
- Music cue
- Micro-reward

TOOL 4: The 90-Day Habit Tracker

Track your daily execution for 90 days. Mark each day:

- ✓ = Completed full action
- ½ = Completed tiny/emergency version only
- X = Missed completely

REMEMBER THE TWO-DAY RULE: You can miss one day. You cannot miss two days in a row.

MY HABIT: _____

MONTH 1 (Days 1-30)

Week 1: ___ ___ ___ ___ ___ ___ ___

Week 2: ___ ___ ___ ___ ___ ___ ___

Week 3: ___ ___ ___ ___ ___ ___ ___

Week 4: ___ ___ ___ ___ ___ ___ ___

Days 29-30: ___ ___

MONTH 2 (Days 31-60)

Week 5: ___ ___ ___ ___ ___ ___ ___

Week 6: ___ ___ ___ ___ ___ ___ ___

Week 7: ___ ___ ___ ___ ___ ___ ___

Week 8: ___ ___ ___ ___ ___ ___ ___

Days 59-60: ___ ___

STEPHEN RUE

MONTH 3 (Days 61-90)

Week 9: ___ ___ ___ ___ ___ ___ ___

Week 10: ___ ___ ___ ___ ___ ___ ___

Week 11: ___ ___ ___ ___ ___ ___ ___

Week 12: ___ ___ ___ ___ ___ ___ ___

Days 89-90: ___ ___

COMPLETION STATS:

Total ✓ days: _____ (Goal: 85+/90 = 94% completion rate)

Total ½ days: _____ (These count! You proved your identity.)

Total X days: _____ (Keep under 5 total, 0 consecutive pairs)

Longest streak: _____ days

APPENDIX TOOL 4

TOOL 4: The 90-Day Habit Tracker

Track your daily execution for 90 days. Mark each day:
- ✓ = Completed full action
- X = Missed completely
- ½ = Completed tiny/emergency version only

REMEMBER THE TWO-DAY RULE. You can miss one day. You cannot miss two days in a row.

MY HABIT: _____

MONTH 1 (Days 1-30)
- Week 1: ☐☐☐☐☐☐☐
- Week 2: ☐☐☐☐☐☐☐
- Week 3: ☐☐☐☐☐☐☐
- Days 29-30: ☐☐

MONTH 2 (Days 31-60)
- Week 5: ☐☐☐☐☐☐☐
- Week 6: ☐☐☐☐☐☐☐
- Week 7: ☐☐☐☐☐☐☐
- Days 59-60: ☐☐

MONTH 2 (Days 31-60)
- Week 9: ☐☐☐☐☐☐☐
- Week 10: ☐☐☐☐☐☐☐
- Week 11: ☐☐☐☐☐☐☐
- Days 59-60: ☐☐

MONTH 3 (Days 61-90)
- Week 9: ☐☐☐☐☐☐☐
- Week 10: ☐☐☐☐☐☐☐
- Week 11: ☐☐☐☐☐☐☐
- Days 89-90: ☐☐

COMPLETION STATS:
- Total ✓ days: _____ (Goal: 85+/90 = 94% completion rate)
- Total ½ days: _____ (These count! You proved your identity.)
- Total X days: _____ (Keep under 5 total, 0 consecutive pairs)
- Longest streak: _____ days

TOOL 5: The Emergency Mini-Habit Planner

Plan your emergency version now, before you need it.

MY FULL HABIT:

_____

_____

MY EMERGENCY MINI-HABIT:

(For sick days, travel, crisis – must be 10-30 seconds max)

_____

_____

EXAMPLES:

- Full: 30-minute workout → Emergency: 5 pushups
- Full: 20-minute meditation → Emergency: 3 deep breaths
- Full: Write 500 words → Emergency: Write one sentence
- Full: Read 20 pages → Emergency: Read one paragraph
- Full: Journal 3 pages → Emergency: Write one gratitude item

WHEN TO USE IT:

- When sick or injured
- When traveling without normal environment
- During major life crisis or disruption
- When you forgot and it's 11:59 PM
- On day 2 after missing day 1 (Two-Day Rule)

Remember: The emergency version still counts. It proves your identity.

APPENDIX TOOL 5

TOOL 5: The Emergency Mini-Habit Planner

Plan your emergency version now, before you need it.

MY FULL HABIT:
_____
_____

MY EMERGENCY MINI-HABIT:
(For sick days, travel, crisis — must be 10-30 seconds max)
_____
_____

EXAMPLES:
- Full: 30-minute workout → Emergency: 5 pushups
- Full: 20-minute meditation → Emergency: 3 deep breaths
- Full: Write 500 words → Emergency: Write one sentence
- Full: Read 20 pages → Emergency: Read one paragraph
- Full: Journal 3 pages → Emergency: Write one gratitude item

WHEN TO USE IT:
- When sick or injured
- When traveling without normal environment
- During major life crisis or disruption
- When you forgot and it's 11:59 PM

Remember: The emergency version still counts. It proves your identity.

TOOL 6: Implementation Intentions Template

Pre-plan your responses to common obstacles using **if-then planning**.

Formula: If [SITUATION], then I will [RESPONSE].

MY HABIT: _____

If I feel like skipping,

then I will: _____

If an obstacle arises (specify: _____),

then I will: _____

If I'm traveling or away from home,

then I will: _____

If I miss a day,

then I will: _____

If someone/something interrupts my signal,

then I will: _____

APPENDIX TOOL 6

TOOL 6: Implementation Intentions Template

Pre-plan your responses to common obstacles using if-then planning.
Formula: If [SITUATION], then I will [RESPONSE].

MY HABIT: _____

If I feel like skipping,
then I will: _____

If an obstacle arises (specify: _____),
then I will: _____

If I'm traveling or away from home, _____
then I will: _____

If I miss a day, _____
then I will: _____

If someone/something interrupts my signal, _____
then I will: _____

COMPLETION STATS:

Total ✓ days: _____ (Goal: 85+/90 = 94% completion rate)   _____
Total ½ days: _____ (These count! You proved your identity.) _____
Total X days: _____ (Keep under 5 total, 0 consecutive pairs) _____

TOOL 7: The Habit Scaling Plan

Plan how you'll increase intensity once the tiny action becomes automatic.

DAYS 1-30: THE TINY ACTION (Master consistency)

My tiny action: _____

Goal: Show up daily, prove identity

DAYS 31-66: SLIGHT INCREASE (Build momentum)

I will increase to: _____

Goal: Add small increment while maintaining consistency

DAYS 67-90: TARGET INTENSITY (Reach full habit)

My full desired habit: _____

Goal: Maintain at target intensity

IMPORTANT REMINDER: Always keep the tiny action as your fallback. On hard days, return to the smallest version. It still counts.

APPENDIX TOOL 7

TOOL 7: The Habit Scaling Plan

Plan how you'll increase intensity once the tiny action becomes automatic.

Formula: If [SITUATION], then I will [RESPONSE].

DAYS 1-30: THE TINY ACTION (Master consistency)
My tiny action: _____
Goal: Show up daily, prove identity

DAYS 31-66: SLIGHT INCREASE (Build momentum)
I will increase to: _____
Goal: Add small increment while maintaining consistency

DAYS 67-90: TARGET INTENSITY (Reach full habit)
My full desired habit: _____
Goal: Maintain at target intensity

DAYS 67-90: TARGET INTENSITY (Reach full habit)
Goal: Maintain at target intensity _____

IMPORTANT REMINDER: Always keep the tiny action as your fallback. On hard days, return to the smallest version. It still counts.

MUST HABITS

Optional Tools

Which Tool Do I Use When?

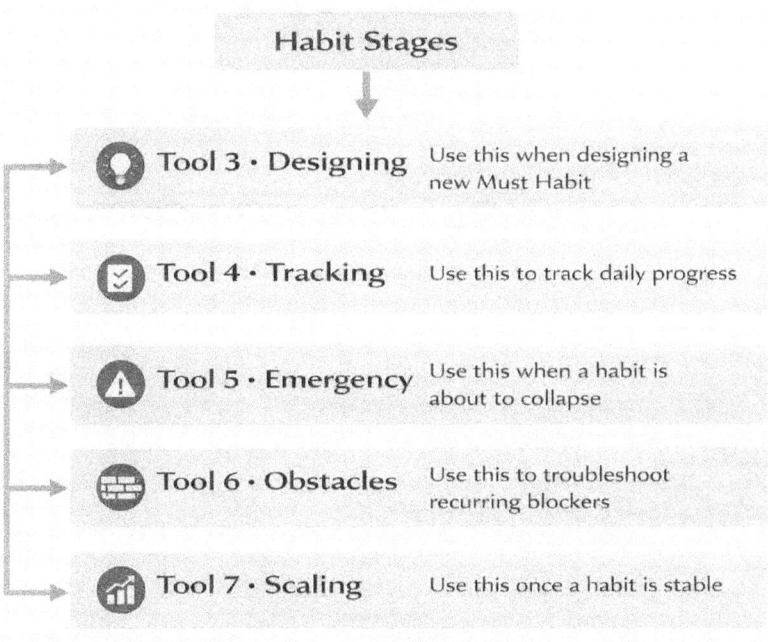

Optional Tool: Common Signal Types

Need help choosing a signal for your habit? Here are common *triggers:*
(Choose ONE)

 Time-Based
- After I wake up
- At 6:00 PM

 Event-Based
- After I pour coffee
- Before I go to bed

 Emotional
- When I feel stressed
- When I'm bored

 Location-Based
- When I sit at my desk
- In the kitchen

 Emotional
- When I feel stressed
- When I'm bored

 Location-Based
- When I sit at my desk
- In the kitchen

APPENDIX B

Quick Reference Guide

Your one-page guide to the complete Must Habits system.

THE MUST HABITS SYSTEM IN 5 MINUTES

STEP 1: ASSESS

- Complete the Circle of Life Assessment (7 domains, 1-10 each)
- Identify your weakest spoke

STEP 2: DECLARE

- Write your I AM Statement: "I am someone who... because..."

STEP 3: DESIGN

- Build your Must Habit Loop:
- Signal: After I [existing behavior]
- Identity: "I am someone who..."
- Tiny Action: [under 2 minutes]
- Evidence: Track + Celebrate

STEP 4: COMMIT

- Mark Day 90 on your calendar
- Plan your emergency mini-habit
- Choose 1-3 advanced strategies

STEP 5: EXECUTE

- Every single day for 90 days:
    1. Signal appears → Pause 3 seconds
    2. Say I AM Statement
    3. Execute tiny action
    4. Mark tracker
    5. Celebrate immediately

CRITICAL RULES

The Two-Day Rule: You can miss one day. You cannot miss two days in a row.

The Sequential Rule: Build ONE habit at a time. Only add the next after 90 days.

The Timeline Rule: 66 days average, 90 days safe bet. Not 21. Not 30.

The Tiny Action Rule: Under 2 minutes. Embarrassingly small. Always executable.

The Emergency Rule: Have a 10-second version ready. It still counts.

THE 3 PHASES YOU'LL EXPERIENCE

Days 1-30: Honeymoon – Motivation high, feels exciting. Don't mistake this for automaticity.

Days 31-66: The Grind – Motivation fades, still feels hard. THIS IS NORMAL. Most quit here. Don't.

Days 67-90: Integration – Starts feeling automatic. Do it without thinking. True automaticity.

QUICK TROUBLESHOOTING

- I forgot → Strengthen signal, add backup reminder
- Too hard → Make tiny action even smaller
- Not motivated → Lean on identity, not motivation
- Broke streak → Execute emergency version today
- No results yet → Trust compound effect, focus on proof

APPENDIX C

Troubleshooting Guide

Common problems and proven solutions.

PROBLEM: "I keep forgetting to do my habit"

Root cause: Weak or inconsistent signal

Solutions:

- Use a signal that happens automatically every day (existing behavior)
- Set phone alarm as backup reminder
- Put visual cue in environment (sticky note, object)
- Stack habit immediately after something you never forget (coffee, brushing teeth)

PROBLEM: "The habit feels too hard, I keep skipping it"

Root cause: Tiny action is not tiny enough

Solutions:

- Make it even smaller (if 5 pushups is hard, do 1)
- Use the 10-second rule (can you do it in 10 seconds?)
- Focus on showing up, not intensity

- Remember: "Put on workout clothes" counts as exercise habit

PROBLEM: "I'm on day 45 and it still doesn't feel automatic"

Root cause: You're in Phase 2 (The Grind)

Solutions:

- This is completely normal – you're not failing, you're early
- Day 45 is two-thirds through the Grind phase
- Automaticity happens around day 66 (you're 3 weeks away)
- Keep showing up – the neural pathway is building invisibly

PROBLEM: "I broke my streak and feel like giving up"

Root cause: Catastrophizing one missed day

Solutions:

- Use the Two-Day Rule: one miss is human, just don't miss tomorrow
- Execute emergency mini-habit today (even 10 seconds)
- The Comeback Formula: Acknowledge → Diagnose → Execute → Recommit
- One break doesn't erase progress – the neural pathway remains

PROBLEM: "I've done this for 60 days and see no results"

Root cause: Results lag behind actions (compound effect)

Solutions:

- Focus on the process, not the outcome
- Ask: "Did I prove my identity today?" not "Did I get results?"
- The payoff is delayed but guaranteed (compounding)
- Small gains accumulate – trust the system

PROBLEM: "Life got chaotic"

Solution: Scale to emergency mini-habit. Maintain identity even if reduced.

PROBLEM: "Want multiple habits faster"

Solution: Sequential beats simultaneous. 90% fail with multiple, 70-80% succeed with one.

PROBLEM: "Environment makes this impossible"

Solution: Redesign environment. Make good habits obvious, bad habits invisible.

APPENDIX D

Resources and References

References

Aarts, H., & Dijksterhuis, A. (2000). Habits as knowledge structures: Automaticity in goal-directed behavior. Journal of Personality and Social Psychology, 78(1), 53–63. https://doi.org/10.1037/0022-3514.78.1.53

Adams, C. D. (1982). Variations in the sensitivity of instrumental responding to reinforcer devaluation. Quarterly Journal of Experimental Psychology Section B, 34(2), 77–98. https://doi.org/10.1080/14640748208400878

Ajzen, I. (1991). The theory of planned behavior. Organizational Behavior and Human Decision Processes, 50(2), 179–211. https://doi.org/10.1016/0749-5978(91)90020-T

Ajzen, I. (2002). Residual effects of past on later behavior: Habituation and reasoned action perspectives. Personality and Social Psychology Review, 6(2), 107–122. https://doi.org/10.1207/S15327957PSPR0602_02

Armitage, C. J. (2005). Can the theory of planned behavior predict the maintenance of physical activity? Health Psychology, 24(3), 235–245. https://doi.org/10.1037/0278-6133.24.3.235

Aunger, R., Schmidt, W.-P., Ranpura, A., Coombes, Y., Maina, P. M., Matiko, C. N., & Curtis, V. (2010). Three kinds of psychological determinants for hand-washing behaviour in Kenya. Social Science & Medicine, 70(3), 383–391. https://doi.org/10.1016/j.socscimed.2009.10.038

Bandura, A. (1977). Self-efficacy: Toward a unifying theory of behavioral change. Psychological Review, 84(2), 191–215. https://doi.org/10.1037/0033-295X.84.2.191

Bandura, A. (1997). Self-efficacy: The exercise of control. W. H. Freeman.

Bargh, J. A. (1994). The four horsemen of automaticity: Awareness, intention, efficiency, and control in social cognition. In R. S. Wyer Jr. & T. K. Srull (Eds.), Handbook of social cognition (2nd ed., Vol. 1, pp. 1–40). Lawrence Erlbaum Associates.

Bargh, J. A., & Chartrand, T. L. (1999). The unbearable automaticity of being. American Psychologist, 54(7), 462–479. https://doi.org/10.1037/0003-066X.54.7.462

Baumeister, R. F. (1998). The self. In D. T. Gilbert, S. T. Fiske, & G. Lindzey (Eds.), The handbook of social psychology (4th ed., Vol. 1, pp. 680–740). McGraw-Hill.

Baumeister, R. F., Bratslavsky, E., Muraven, M., & Tice, D. M. (1998). Ego depletion: Is the active self a limited resource? Journal of Personality and Social Psychology, 74(5), 1252–1265. https://doi.org/10.1037/0022-3514.74.5.1252

Baumeister, R. F., Gailliot, M., DeWall, C. N., & Oaten, M. (2006). Self-regulation and personality: How interventions increase regulatory success, and how depletion moderates the effects of traits on behavior. Journal of Personality, 74(6), 1773–1801. https://doi.org/10.1111/j.1467-6494.2006.00428.x

Baumeister, R. F., Heatherton, T. F., & Tice, D. M. (1994). Losing control: How and why people fail at self-regulation. Academic Press.

Baumeister, R. F., & Tierney, J. (2011). Willpower: Rediscovering the greatest human strength. Penguin Press.

Baumeister, R. F., Vohs, K. D., & Tice, D. M. (2007). The strength model of self-control. Current Directions in Psychological Science, 16(6), 351–355. https://doi.org/10.1111/j.1467-8721.2007.00534.x

Bem, D. J. (1972). Self-perception theory. In L. Berkowitz (Ed.), Advances in experimental social psychology (Vol. 6, pp. 1–62). Academic Press.

Boucher, H. C., & Kofos, M. N. (2012). The idea of money counteracts ego depletion effects. Journal of Experimental Social Psychology, 48(4), 804–810. https://doi.org/10.1016/j.jesp.2012.02.003

Cialdini, R. B. (2006). Influence: The psychology of persuasion (Rev. ed.). Harper Business.

Clear, J. (2018). Atomic habits: An easy & proven way to build good habits & break bad ones. Avery.

Cunningham, M. R., & Baumeister, R. F. (2016). How to make nothing out of something: Analyses of the impact of study sampling and statistical interpretation in misleading meta-analytic conclusions. Frontiers in Psychology, 7, Article 1639. https://doi.org/10.3389/fpsyg.2016.01639

Danziger, S., Levav, J., & Avnaim-Pesso, L. (2011). Extraneous factors in judicial decisions. Proceedings of the National Academy of Sciences, 108(17), 6889–6892. https://doi.org/10.1073/pnas.1018033108

de Bruijn, G. J. (2010). Understanding college students' fruit consumption: Integrating habit strength in the theory of planned behaviour. Appetite, 54(1), 16–22. https://doi.org/10.1016/j.appet.2009.08.007

de Bruijn, G. J., & Gardner, B. (2011). Active commuting and habit strength: An interactive and discriminant analyses approach. American Journal of Health Promotion, 25(3), e27–e36. https://doi.org/10.4278/ajhp.090521-QUAN-170

de Wit, S., & Dickinson, A. (2009). Associative theories of goal-directed behaviour: A case for animal–human translational models. Psychological Research, 73(4), 463–476. https://doi.org/10.1007/s00426-009-0230-6

Dickinson, A. (1985). Actions and habits: The development of behavioural autonomy. Philosophical Transactions of the Royal Society of London B, 308(1135), 67–78. https://doi.org/10.1098/rstb.1985.0010

Duhigg, C. (2012). The power of habit: Why we do what we do in life and business. Random House.

Dweck, C. S. (2006). Mindset: The new psychology of success. Random House.

Evans, D. R., Boggero, I. A., & Segerstrom, S. C. (2016). The nature of self-regulatory fatigue and "ego depletion": Lessons from physical fatigue. Personality and Social Psychology Review, 20(4), 291–310. https://doi.org/10.1177/1088868315597841

Fazio, R. H., Sherman, S. J., & Herr, P. M. (1982). The feature-positive effect in the self-perception process: Does not doing matter as much as doing? Journal of Personality and Social Psychology, 42(3), 404–411. https://doi.org/10.1037/0022-3514.42.3.404

Fife-Schaw, C., Sheeran, P., & Norman, P. (2007). Simulating behaviour change interventions based on the theory of planned behaviour: Impacts on intention and action. British Journal of Social Psychology, 46(1), 43–68. https://doi.org/10.1348/014466605X85906

Finkenauer, C., Buyukcan-Tetik, A., Baumeister, R. F., Schoemaker, K., Bartels, M., & Vohs, K. D. (2015). Out of control: Identifying the role of self-control strength in family violence. Current Directions in Psychological Science, 24(4), 261–266. https://doi.org/10.1177/0963721415570730

Fogg, B. J. (2002). Persuasive technology: Using computers to change what we think and do. Morgan Kaufmann.

Fogg, B. J. (2009). A behavior model for persuasive design. In Proceedings of the 4th International Conference on Persuasive Technology (Article 40). ACM. https://doi.org/10.1145/1541948.1541999

Fogg, B. J. (2019). Tiny habits: The small changes that change everything. Houghton Mifflin Harcourt.

Friese, M., Frankenbach, J., Job, V., & Loschelder, D. D. (2017). Does self-control training improve self-control? A meta-analysis. Perspectives on Psychological Science, 12(6), 1077–1099. https://doi.org/10.1177/1745691617697076

Gailliot, M. T., Baumeister, R. F., DeWall, C. N., Maner, J. K., Plant, E. A., Tice, D. M., Brewer, L. E., & Schmeichel, B. J. (2007). Self-control relies on glucose as a limited energy source: Willpower is more than a metaphor. Journal of Personality and Social Psychology, 92(2), 325–336. https://doi.org/10.1037/0022-3514.92.2.325

Gardner, B., Abraham, C., Lally, P., & de Bruijn, G. J. (2012). Towards parsimony in habit measurement: Testing the convergent and predictive validity of an automaticity subscale of the self-report habit index. International Journal of Behavioral

Nutrition and Physical Activity, 9, Article 102. https://doi.org/10.1186/1479-5868-9-102

Gardner, B., de Bruijn, G. J., & Lally, P. (2011). A systematic review and meta-analysis of applications of the self-report habit index to nutrition and physical activity behaviours. Annals of Behavioral Medicine, 42(2), 174–187. https://doi.org/10.1007/s12160-011-9282-0

Gardner, B., Lally, P., & Wardle, J. (2012). Making health habitual: The psychology of habit-formation and general practice. British Journal of General Practice, 62(605), 664–666. https://doi.org/10.3399/bjgp12X659466

Gollwitzer, P. M. (1999). Implementation intentions: Strong effects of simple plans. American Psychologist, 54(7), 493–503. https://doi.org/10.1037/0003-066X.54.7.493

Gollwitzer, P. M., & Brandstätter, V. (1997). Implementation intentions and effective goal pursuit. Journal of Personality and Social Psychology, 73(1), 186–199. https://doi.org/10.1037/0022-3514.73.1.186

Gollwitzer, P. M., & Sheeran, P. (2006). Implementation intentions and goal achievement: A meta-analysis of effects and processes. Advances in Experimental Social Psychology, 38, 69–119. https://doi.org/10.1016/S0065-2601(06)38002-1

Gottfredson, M. R., & Hirschi, T. (1990). A general theory of crime. Stanford University Press.

Graybiel, A. M. (2008). Habits, rituals, and the evaluative brain. Annual Review of Neuroscience, 31, 359–387. https://doi.org/10.1146/annurev.neuro.29.051605.112851

Graybiel, A. M., & Smith, K. S. (2014). Good habits, bad habits. Scientific American, 310(6), 38–43. https://doi.org/10.1038/scientificamerican0614-38

Guise, S. (2013). Mini habits: Smaller habits, bigger results. Selective Entertainment.

Hagger, M. S., & Chatzisarantis, N. L. D. (2014). An integrated behavior change model for physical activity. Exercise and Sport Sciences Reviews, 42(2), 62–69. https://doi.org/10.1249/JES.0000000000000008

Hagger, M. S., Chatzisarantis, N. L. D., Alberts, H., Anggono, C. O., Batailler, C., Birt, A. R., Brand, R., Brandt, M. J., Brewer, G., Bruyneel, S., Calvillo, D. P., Campbell, W. K., Cannon, P. R., Carlucci, M., Carruth, N. P., Cheung, T., Crowell, A., De Ridder, D. T. D., Dewitte, S., ... Zwienenberg, M. (2016). A multilab preregistered replication of the ego-depletion effect. Perspectives on Psychological Science, 11(4), 546–573. https://doi.org/10.1177/1745691616652873

Hagger, M. S., Wood, C., Stiff, C., & Chatzisarantis, N. L. D. (2010). Ego depletion and the strength model of self-control: A meta-analysis. Psychological Bulletin, 136(4), 495–525. https://doi.org/10.1037/a0019486

Hardy, D. (2010). The compound effect. Vanguard Press.

Heath, C., & Heath, D. (2010). Switch: How to change things when change is hard. Broadway Books.

Inzlicht, M., & Schmeichel, B. J. (2012). What is ego depletion? Toward a mechanistic revision of the resource model of self-control. Perspectives on Psychological Science, 7(5), 450–463. https://doi.org/10.1177/1745691612454134

Inzlicht, M., Schmeichel, B. J., & Macrae, C. N. (2014). Why self-control seems (but may not be) limited. Trends in Cognitive Sciences, 18(3), 127–133. https://doi.org/10.1016/j.tics.2013.12.009

James, W. (1890). The principles of psychology. Henry Holt and Company.

Ji, M. F., & Wood, W. (2007). Purchase and consumption habits: Not necessarily what you intend. Journal of Consumer Psychology, 17(4), 261–276. https://doi.org/10.1016/S1057-7408(07)70037-2

Job, V., Dweck, C. S., & Walton, G. M. (2010). Ego depletion—Is it all in your head? Implicit theories about willpower affect self-regulation. Psychological Science, 21(11), 1686–1693. https://doi.org/10.1177/0956797610384745

Job, V., Walton, G. M., Bernecker, K., & Dweck, C. S. (2015). Implicit theories about willpower predict self-regulation and grades in everyday life. Journal of Personality and Social Psychology, 108(4), 637–647. https://doi.org/10.1037/pspp0000014

Kahneman, D. (2011). Thinking, fast and slow. Farrar, Straus and Giroux.

Keller, J., Kwasnicka, D., Klaiber, P., Sichert, L., Lally, P., & Fleig, L. (2021). Habit formation following routine-based versus time-based cue planning: A randomized controlled trial. British Journal of Health Psychology, 26(3), 807–824. https://doi.org/10.1111/bjhp.12504

Kilb, M., & Labudek, S. (2022). Effects of a habitual behavior's reinforcer value on habit expression. Journal of Experimental Psychology: Animal Learning and Cognition, 48(4), 377–393. https://doi.org/10.1037/xan0000329

Lally, P., Chipperfield, A., & Wardle, J. (2008). Healthy habits: Efficacy of simple advice on weight control based on a habit-formation model. International Journal of Obesity, 32(4), 700–707. https://doi.org/10.1038/sj.ijo.0803771

Lally, P., & Gardner, B. (2013). Promoting habit formation. Health Psychology Review, 7(Suppl. 1), S137–S158. https://doi.org/10.1080/17437199.2011.603640

Lally, P., van Jaarsveld, C. H. M., Potts, H. W. W., & Wardle, J. (2010). How are habits formed: Modelling habit formation in the real world. European Journal of Social Psychology, 40(6), 998–1009. https://doi.org/10.1002/ejsp.674

Lally, P., Wardle, J., & Gardner, B. (2011). Experiences of habit formation: A qualitative study. Psychology, Health & Medicine, 16(4), 484–489. https://doi.org/10.1080/13548506.2011.555774

Linder, J. A., Doctor, J. N., Friedberg, M. W., Reyes Nieva, H., Birks, C., Meeker, D., & Fox, C. R. (2014). Time of day and the decision to prescribe antibiotics. JAMA Internal Medicine, 174(12), 2029–2031. https://doi.org/10.1001/jamainternmed.2014.5225

Maltz, M. (1960). Psycho-cybernetics. Prentice-Hall.

Michie, S., Abraham, C., Whittington, C., McAteer, J., & Gupta, S. (2009). Effective techniques in healthy eating and physical activity interventions: A meta-regression. Health Psychology, 28(6), 690–701. https://doi.org/10.1037/a0016136

Milkman, K. L., Beshears, J., Choi, J. J., Laibson, D., & Madrian, B. C. (2011). Using implementation intentions prompts to enhance influenza vaccination rates. Proceedings of the National Academy of Sciences, 108(26), 10415–10420. https://doi.org/10.1073/pnas.1103170108

Mischel, W., Shoda, Y., & Rodriguez, M. L. (1989). Delay of gratification in children. Science, 244(4907), 933–938. https://doi.org/10.1126/science.2658056

Muraven, M. (2010). Building self-control strength: Practicing self-control leads to improved self-control performance. Journal of Experimental Social Psychology, 46(2), 465–468. https://doi.org/10.1016/j.jesp.2009.12.011

Muraven, M., & Baumeister, R. F. (2000). Self-regulation and depletion of limited resources: Does self-control resemble a muscle? Psychological Bulletin, 126(2), 247–259. https://doi.org/10.1037/0033-2909.126.2.247

Muraven, M., Shmueli, D., & Burkley, E. (2006). Conserving self-control strength. Journal of Personality and Social Psychology, 91(3), 524–537. https://doi.org/10.1037/0022-3514.91.3.524

Muraven, M., Tice, D. M., & Baumeister, R. F. (1998). Self-control as a limited resource: Regulatory depletion patterns. Journal of Personality and Social Psychology, 74(3), 774–789. https://doi.org/10.1037/0022-3514.74.3.774

Neal, D. T., Wood, W., & Quinn, J. M. (2006). Habits—A repeat performance. Current Directions in Psychological Science, 15(4), 198–202. https://doi.org/10.1111/j.1467-8721.2006.00435.x

Neal, D. T., Wood, W., Wu, M., & Kurlander, D. (2011). The pull of the past: When do habits persist despite conflict with motives? Personality and Social Psychology Bulletin, 37(11), 1428–1437. https://doi.org/10.1177/0146167211419863

Oaten, M., & Cheng, K. (2006). Longitudinal gains in self-regulation from regular physical exercise. British Journal of Health Psychology, 11(4), 717–733. https://doi.org/10.1348/135910706X96481

Orbell, S., & Verplanken, B. (2010). The automatic component of habit in health behavior: Habit as cue-contingent automaticity. Health Psychology, 29(4), 374–383. https://doi.org/10.1037/a0019596

Ouellette, J. A., & Wood, W. (1998). Habit and intention in everyday life: The multiple processes by which past behavior predicts future behavior. Psychological Bulletin, 124(1), 54–74. https://doi.org/10.1037/0033-2909.124.1.54

Phillips, L. A., & Gardner, B. (2016). Habitual exercise instigation (vs. execution) predicts healthy adults' exercise frequency. Health Psychology, 35(1), 69–77. https://doi.org/10.1037/hea0000249

Phillips, L. A., & Mullan, B. A. (2023). Ramifications of behavioural complexity for habit conceptualisation. In B. Verplanken (Ed.), The psychology of habit (pp. 165–182). Springer.

Pocheptsova, A., Amir, O., Dhar, R., & Baumeister, R. F. (2009). Deciding without resources: Resource depletion and choice in context. Journal of Marketing Research, 46(3), 344–355. https://doi.org/10.1509/jmkr.46.3.344

Quinn, J. M., Pascoe, A., Wood, W., & Neal, D. T. (2010). Can't control yourself? Monitor those bad habits. Personality and Social Psychology Bulletin, 36(4), 499–511. https://doi.org/10.1177/0146167209360665

Rhodes, R. E., de Bruijn, G. J., & Matheson, D. H. (2010). Habit in the physical activity domain: Integration with intention temporal stability and action control. Journal of Sport & Exercise Psychology, 32(1), 84–98. https://doi.org/10.1123/jsep.32.1.84

Richeson, J. A., & Shelton, J. N. (2003). When prejudice does not pay: Effects of interracial contact on executive function. Psychological Science, 14(3), 287–290. https://doi.org/10.1111/1467-9280.03437

Rothman, A. J., Sheeran, P., & Wood, W. (2009). Reflective and automatic processes in the initiation and maintenance of dietary change. Annals of Behavioral Medicine, 38(Suppl. 1), S4–S17. https://doi.org/10.1007/s12160-009-9118-3

Rue, S. (2025). Must: Becoming the Person You Are Meant to Be. Houndstooth Press

Schmeichel, B. J., Vohs, K. D., & Baumeister, R. F. (2003). Intellectual performance and ego depletion: Role of the self in logical reasoning and other information processing. Journal of Personality and Social Psychology, 85(1), 33–46. https://doi.org/10.1037/0022-3514.85.1.33

Schultz, W. (1998). Predictive reward signal of dopamine neurons. Journal of Neurophysiology, 80(1), 1–27. https://doi.org/10.1152/jn.1998.80.1.1

Schultz, W. (2015). Neuronal reward and decision signals: From theories to data. Physiological Reviews, 95(3), 853–951. https://doi.org/10.1152/physrev.00023.2014

Schwarzer, R. (1992). Self-efficacy in the adoption and maintenance of health behaviors: Theoretical approaches and a new model. In R. Schwarzer (Ed.), Self-efficacy: Thought control of action (pp. 217–243). Hemisphere.

Segar, M. L. (2022). Sustainable behavior change requires far more than habit formation. American Journal of Lifestyle Medicine, 16(3), 304–307. https://doi.org/10.1177/15598276221089037

Tangney, J. P., Baumeister, R. F., & Boone, A. L. (2004). High self-control predicts good adjustment, less pathology, better grades, and interpersonal success. Journal of Personality, 72(2), 271–322. https://doi.org/10.1111/j.0022-3506.2004.00263.x

Tetlock, P. E. (1983). Accountability and complexity of thought. Journal of Personality and Social Psychology, 45(1), 74–83. https://doi.org/10.1037/0022-3514.45.1.74

Tetlock, P. E. (1985). Accountability: A social check on the fundamental attribution error. Social Psychology Quarterly, 48(3), 227–236. https://doi.org/10.2307/3033683

Tetlock, P. E., & Boettger, R. (1989). Accountability: A social magnifier of the dilution effect. Journal of Personality and Social Psychology, 57(3), 388–398. https://doi.org/10.1037/0022-3514.57.3.388

Tice, D. M., Baumeister, R. F., Shmueli, D., & Muraven, M. (2007). Restoring the self: Positive affect helps improve self-regulation following ego depletion. Journal of Experimental Social Psychology, 43(3), 379–384. https://doi.org/10.1016/j.jesp.2006.05.007

Triandis, H. C. (1977). Interpersonal behavior. Brooks/Cole.

Verplanken, B. (2006). Beyond frequency: Habit as mental construct. British Journal of Social Psychology, 45(3), 639–656. https://doi.org/10.1348/014466605X49122

Verplanken, B., & Aarts, H. (1999). Habit, attitude, and planned behaviour: Is habit an empty construct or an interesting case of goal-directed automaticity? European Review of Social Psychology, 10(1), 101–134. https://doi.org/10.1080/14792779943000035

Verplanken, B., & Orbell, S. (2003). Reflections on past behavior: A self-report index of habit strength. Journal of Applied Social Psychology, 33(6), 1313–1330. https://doi.org/10.1111/j.1559-1816.2003.tb01951.x

Verplanken, B., & Wood, W. (2006). Interventions to break and create consumer habits. Journal of Public Policy & Marketing, 25(1), 90–103. https://doi.org/10.1509/jppm.25.1.90

Vohs, K. D., Baumeister, R. F., Schmeichel, B. J., Twenge, J. M., Nelson, N. M., & Tice, D. M. (2008). Making choices impairs subsequent self-control: A limited-resource account of decision making, self-regulation, and active initiative. Journal of Personality and Social Psychology, 94(5), 883–898. https://doi.org/10.1037/0022-3514.94.5.883

Vohs, K. D., & Heatherton, T. F. (2000). Self-regulatory failure: A resource-depletion approach. Psychological Science, 11(3), 249–254. https://doi.org/10.1111/1467-9280.00250

Webb, T. L., & Sheeran, P. (2006). Does changing behavioral intentions engender behavior change? A meta-analysis of the experimental evidence. Psychological Bulletin, 132(2), 249–268. https://doi.org/10.1037/0033-2909.132.2.249

Wood, W., & Neal, D. T. (2007). A new look at habits and the habit-goal interface. Psychological Review, 114(4), 843–863. https://doi.org/10.1037/0033-295X.114.4.843

Wood, W., & Neal, D. T. (2009). The habitual consumer. Journal of Consumer Psychology, 19(4), 579–592. https://doi.org/10.1016/j.jcps.2009.08.003

Wood, W., & Quinn, J. M. (2005). Habits and the structure of motivation in everyday life. In J. P. Forgas, K. D. Williams, & S. M. Laham (Eds.), Social motivation: Conscious and unconscious processes (pp. 55–70). Cambridge University Press.

Wood, W., Quinn, J. M., & Kashy, D. A. (2002). Habits in everyday life: Thought, emotion, and action. Journal of Personality and Social Psychology, 83(6), 1281–1297. https://doi.org/10.1037/0022-3514.83.6.1281

Wood, W., Tam, L., & Witt, M. G. (2005). Changing circumstances, disrupting habits. Journal of Personality and Social Psychology, 88(6), 918–933. https://doi.org/10.1037/0022-3514.88.6.918

We continue to update resources at
MustHabits.com/Resources

ABOUT THE AUTHOR

STEPHEN RUE is a personal development expert, award-winning author, speaker, and certified trauma-recovery life coach whose mission is to help others overcome adversity and build extraordinary lives.

Stephen's academic credentials reflect a lifelong commitment to understanding human potential. He earned his Bachelor of Business Administration from Southern Methodist University and his Master of Business Administration and Juris Doctor from Loyola University New Orleans. He holds a certificate in Negotiation and Leadership from Harvard Law School and is a certified trauma-recovery life coach. He is currently completing his doctorate in Organizational Leadership from National University, with his dissertation focused on well-being and human flourishing.

For nearly four decades, Stephen has practiced family law in New Orleans, earning the distinction of being voted "Best Attorney" by Gambit Weekly's Best of New Orleans Readers' Poll. His legal career has given him a front-row seat to human behavior—what drives people, what holds them back, and what transforms them.

His personal journey through adversity—including the loss of his stepfather to suicide when Stephen was just eleven years old—became the catalyst for his life's work. Watching his mother's remarkable resilience in the face of tragedy taught him that transformation is possible, that identity shapes behavior, and that the right habits can rebuild a life from the ground up.

Stephen is the author of the acclaimed Must Personal Development series:

- Must: Becoming the Person You Are Meant to Be
- Must Mindset: The Psychology of Personal Transformation
- Must Habits: The Science of Sustainable Change
- Must Purpose: Building a Life of Meaning
- Must Love: Five Non-Negotiable Standards for Love That Lasts

His books have received numerous national and international awards, including:

- Winner – Paris Book Festival Award
- Gold Medal – Global Book Award
- Winner – Pinnacle Book Achievement Award
- Winner – Southern California Book Festival Award
- Winner – New England Book Festival Award

Stephen's work blends rigorous research in psychology, neuroscience, and human behavior with practical wisdom gained from decades of professional experience and personal transformation. His insights have helped thousands discover their identity, clarify their purpose, build lasting habits, and create lives of meaning.

Connect with the author:
Website: www.MustHabits.com
Author Website: StephenRue.Live
Email: Stephen@StephenRue.com
Instagram: SouthernFriedLawyer
Twitter: @StephenRue

ACKNOWLEDGMENTS

I want to express my sincere appreciation to the researchers, scholars, and practitioners whose work in behavioral science, psychology, neuroscience, and habit formation informed and strengthened this manuscript. Their rigorous inquiry and commitment to evidence-based understanding made this work possible.

I am also grateful to my academic colleagues and mentors for their thoughtful dialogue, critical feedback, and shared dedication to intellectual integrity. Their perspectives sharpened both the clarity and credibility of this work.

A FINAL WORD

You've reached the end of this book.

But you're standing at the beginning of something far more important: your transformation.

Somewhere in these pages, you discovered a habit that resonated. A domain that needs strengthening. An identity you want to prove.

The question now is simple: Will you begin?

Ninety days from today, you could have one automatic habit. One strengthened spoke. One area of your life transformed from neglect to thriving.

One hundred eighty days from today, two habits. Two spokes. Two domains.

Seven hundred thirty days from today, your entire Circle of Life could be balanced. Every spoke strong. The wheel rolling smoothly.

Or nothing changes.

You go back to your old patterns. The broken wheel keeps wobbling. The gap between who you are and who you could be stays wide.

The choice is yours.

But remember this:

Transformation doesn't require a breakthrough moment. It doesn't require perfect conditions. It doesn't require more time, more willpower, or more motivation.

It requires one thing:

Tomorrow morning, when your signal appears, pause for three seconds. Say your I AM Statement. Execute your tiny action. Mark your tracker. Celebrate.

That's it.

Do that ninety times, and the person you're becoming becomes who you are.

You are one tiny action away from proof.

You are ninety tiny actions away from transformation.

The system works.

Now it's your turn to prove it.

Begin.

REFERENCES & ONGOING RESEARCH UPDATES

This book draws from decades of psychological research, behavioral science, leadership theory, human performance studies, and spiritual development literature. The works listed in the References section represent many of the foundational books, peer-reviewed studies, and theoretical frameworks that support the principles of identity-based goal setting, habit formation, motivation, and personal transformation presented in *Must Habits*.

Because science evolves, and because new studies continue to refine what we know about human behavior, habit formation, resilience, implementation intentions, purpose, identity, and motivation, **updated research—along with expanded reading recommendations, new models, and supplemental tools—will be maintained at:**

MustHabits.com/Resources

There you will find:

- Updated studies in psychology, neuroscience, and behavioral change
- Expanded reading lists for identity work, habit formation, and resilience

- Downloadable worksheets and templates
- Visual models and diagrams from the book
- Supplemental exercises and case studies
- Bonus content that continues to grow over time

This ensures that *Must Habits* remains a **living, evolving system**, grounded in the most current research and best practices.

THANK YOU, AND NEXT STEPS

If this book has encouraged or helped you, **would you take a moment to leave a review?**

https://a.co/d/4yqp4Y3

Your feedback makes a real difference and helps other readers discover this work. You can share your thoughts on Amazon.com, Goodreads.com, Barnes & Noble, or your preferred bookseller, and consider sharing or gifting this book to someone who might benefit from it. To continue your journey, visit **MustHabits.com** and **StephenRue.Live** for more resources, events, and tools in the Must Personal Development series.

Thank you for being part of this work and for supporting these books.

THE MUST PERSONAL DEVELOPMENT SERIES

Continuing Your Journey Beyond Court

When the hearings end and the orders are signed, your case may be closed—but your life is not. Surviving a high-conflict custody battle changes you. The real work afterward is rebuilding who you are, how you live, and what you are moving toward next.

If you are ready to heal, grow, and design a future that is not defined by conflict, The Must Personal Development Series is designed to walk beside you.

The Must Personal Development Series

by Stephen Rue

Must: Becoming the Person You Are Meant to Be

Your foundation. This book helps you uncover your Must Identity, challenge old narratives, clarify your core values and standards, and step into the person you are meant to be—beyond the courtroom and the conflict.

https://www.StephenRue.Live

Must Goals: The Art and Science of Authentic Goal-Setting for Lasting Change

Your method. Here you learn to create goals rooted in identity instead of fear, pressure, or survival mode, using the I AM SMART TO ACT™ framework and research-backed tools for lasting change in every area of your life.

https://www.StephenRue.Live

The Must Book Guided Journal

Your weekly integration. A structured space to reflect, recalibrate, and live your Must Identity week by week, with prompts that help you process what you have been through and move toward the life you want to build.

Must Year Your Best Year of Becoming – A 365-Day Journey of Identity, Growth, and Habits

Your daily practice. A 365-day companion that keeps you grounded, focused, and intentional—one small decision at a time—as you create stability, purpose, and joy for yourself and your children.

Each book stands on its own. Together, they form a practical roadmap from crisis and survival to clarity, identity, and a more aligned way of living.

Your custody case may have forced you into this fight. What you do next is your choice. If you are ready to keep rebuilding—with purpose instead of panic and with identity instead of just reaction—the Must Personal Development Series is here to support your next chapter.

www.ingramcontent.com/pod-product-compliance
Lightning Source LLC
Chambersburg PA
CBHW020853090426
42736CB00008B/356